Nuts

JOKE BOOK 2

This is a Carlton Book

Published by The Carlton Publishing Group
20 Mortimer Street
London W1T 3JW

ISBN 978-1-84442-771-0

10 9 8 7 6 5 4 3 2 1

Typesetting by e-type, Liverpool

Printed in Great Britain

Nuts

JOKE BOOK 2

CARLTON
BOOKS

A message from
THE Nuts TEAM

Have you heard the one about the Dutch priest and the 12-inch carrot? No, neither have we. And to be honest, it doesn't sound like it'll be very funny, which is why you won't be finding it in the Nuts Joke Book Mark 2. What you will be finding are hundreds of the very funniest jokes we at Team Nuts have ever heard – in fact, if it's funny and it's not here, then it must've been in the first Nuts Joke Book. That's how authoritative this second jokes compendium is.

Yes, since the release of the first best-selling Nuts Joke Book, our top comedy boffins have been locked in a humour-tight room and subjected to a barrage of the most hilarious jokes in the world, with a view to whittling our vast stockpile of gags down to one book-sized serving. After months of one-liners, puns, naughty punchlines and unlikely scenarios involving dogs, we believe that we've assembled the single greatest gathering of gags the world has ever seen. And that's not a claim we make lightly. Although, we made it there lightly enough. Prepare your sides for serious pain – the Nuts Joke Book is back.

From the readers of NUTS

Air traffic self-control

A mother and her young son are on a long-haul flight to America. The son, looking out of the plane's window, turns to his mum and says, "Mum, if big dogs have baby dogs and big cats have baby cats, why don't big planes have baby planes?"

Stumped for an answer, the mother suggests that her son ask the stewardess. The boy promptly gets out of his seat and wanders back to the service area.

"Excuse me," the boy says to the stewardess. "If big dogs have baby dogs and big cats have baby cats, why don't big planes have baby planes?"

"Did your mother tell you to ask me that?"

"Yes," he says.

The stewardess whispers in the boy's ear, "Tell your mother it's because British Airways always pulls out on time."

Thanks for your support

A Sunderland season ticket-holder calls up the Stadium of Light and asks "What time does the game start?"

The ticket office replies, "What time can you get here?"

...Is the right answer!

Brian goes to see his supervisor in the front office.

"Boss," he says, "we're doing some heavy house-cleaning at home tomorrow, and my wife needs me to help with the attic and the garage, moving and hauling stuff."

"We're short-handed, Brian," the boss replies. "I can't give you the day off."

"Thanks, boss," says Brian, "I knew I could count on you!"

Tool of the trade

A woman walks into a sex toy store and asks where the vibrators are. "Come this way," the cute woman behind the counter says, gesturing with her finger. "If I could come that way, I wouldn't need the vibrator, would I?" the woman responds.

Body language

A couple, who have been married for years, are making love.
He asks, "Dear, am I hurting you?"
"No," she replies. "But why do you ask?"
"You moved," he says.

Right man for the job

Two MPs are talking late at night in the House of Commons bar.
"How do you choose the right person to back for Prime Minister?" says the younger politician.
"Easy," says the old buffer. "Just adopt the same procedure as you would when choosing a taxi driver."
"What's that?" says the young MP.
"Just decide which one will cost you least and not get you killed."

The first cut is the deepest

Feeling uncertain about his love life, a frog calls up a psychic hotline.
"I can see that you're going to meet a beautiful young girl who will want to know everything about you," the psychic tells the frog.

"That's great," the frog says. "Will I meet this babe at a party?"

"No," the psychic says. "In her biology class next term."

Limited vocabulary

A competition is running on a local radio station.

"Right," says the DJ. "If you can give a word in normal, everyday use that's not in the dictionary then you win £100."

Only one light comes on on the phone banks and the DJ punches it quickly.

"Hi, caller. What's your word?" says the DJ.

"GOAN," says the caller.

"How do you spell that?" says the DJ.

"G-O-A-N," the caller replies.

> **What's the difference between a bad golfer and a bad skydiver?**
> **The golfer goes "Thump..." "DAMN!"**

"Well, that's certainly not in the dictionary, but before you get the money can you tell me how you would use it in a sentence?"

"Goan f*** yoursel..." The DJ cuts him off and apologises to his audience for the bad language. Thankfully, another call comes in and the DJ is relieved to be able to move on.

"What's your word, caller?" he enquires.

"SMEE," says the caller.

"And how do you spell that?" says the DJ.

"S-M-E-E," says the caller.

"Well, you're correct SMEE isn't in the dictionary," says the

DJ, "but before we give you the money can you tell me how you would use that in a sentence?"

"Smee again," says the caller. "Now goan f*** yourself."

When you gotta go...

A doctor says to his patient: "I have bad news and worse news."

"Oh, dear; what's the bad news?" asks the patient.

The doctor replies: "You only have 24 hours to live."

"That's terrible," says the patient. "How can the news possibly be worse?"

The doctor replies: "I've been trying to contact you since yesterday."

Frequent flier

On the first day of university, the students are told some of the rules: "The female dormitory is out of bounds for all male students, as is the male dormitory to the female students. Anybody caught breaking this rule will be fined £20 the first time. Anybody caught breaking this rule the second time will be fined £60. Being caught a third time will cost you £180. Are there any questions?"

A young male student pipes up: "How much for a season ticket?"

Tell me again slowly...

Two blokes are lying in bed when one turns to the other and says, "I don't think much of this wife-swapping."

Balance of probabilities

Paul McCartney claims he's not worried about Heather Mills' accusation of wife-beating. He says, "It'll never stand up in court."

Smart move

God is talking to Adam and Eve one day during the Creation. "Well, you two, I only have a couple more goodies left to hand out before my job is done. Which one of you wants to be able to pee standing up?"

Adam raises his hand and yells, "Me, me, pick me!" So God obliges.

God looks at Eve and says: "Well, sorry, Eve… but it looks like you're stuck with the multiple orgasms."

One-track mind

A man goes to see a psychiatrist, who gives him the inkblot test.

"What does this picture remind you of?" the doctor asks.

"A lesbian nun orgy," the fella replies.

"How about this one?" the shrink asks, holding up another picture.

"A Girls Aloud orgy," the guy says.

After three more pictures, the doctor finally puts down the cards. "You are a sick pervert," he says.

"Me?" the man says indignantly. "You're the one who keeps showing me dirty pictures."

Middle stump

Ladies' man Shane Warne is at an Ashes press conference. An Aussie journalist asks, "What would you do if you only had 30 minutes to live, Shane?"

"Ah, mate," he says, "I'd shag the first thing that moved."

The journalist then asks the same question of Freddie Flintoff: "What would you do if you only had 30 minutes to live?"

Freddie eyes Warnie suspiciously and says, "I'd sit very, very still."

Good manners

Two old women are sitting in their retirement home.

The first woman says, "When my first child was born, my husband bought me a mansion in Jersey."

The second woman says, "Fantastic."

The other woman brags, "When my second child was born my husband bought me a Rolls-Royce."

"Fantastic," the other woman replies.

"And when my third child was born, my husband bought me the most expensive diamond bracelet they had at Tiffany's."

"Fantastic," says the second old lady.

"So what did your husband buy you when your first child was born?" says the bragging old dear.

"He sent me to charm school," the quiet one replies.

"What the hell for?"

"So instead of saying, 'Who gives a shit?' I could learn to say, 'Fantastic.'"

And it was good

God, feeling very proud of himself, tells St Peter that he's just created a 24-hour period of alternating light and darkness on earth. "That's clever, God," says St Peter, "what will you do now?"

"Oh, I think I'll call it a day," replies God.

Late developer

On the first day of primary school, the teacher asks everyone to count to 50. Some count as high as 30 or 40; others can't get past 20, but Wayne counts up to 100 without any mistakes. When he tells his dad how well he did, his dad says, "That's because you're an Aussie, son."

The next day, the teacher asks everyone to recite the alphabet. Most can only make it half-way through without trouble, but Wayne rattles off the letters perfectly. When he brags to his dad about how he did, his dad explains, "That's because you're an Aussie, son."

The next day, after games, the boys hit the showers, and Wayne notices that he is better endowed than anyone else. That night he boasts, "Dad, mine's the biggest of anyone in my class. Is it because I'm an Aussie?"

"No, son," explains his dad. "It's because you're 22."

The Lord's work

An old nun who lives in a convent next to a construction site notices the bad language of the workers, and decides to spend some time with them to correct their ways.

She decides she'll take her lunch, sit with the workers and talk with them, so she puts her sandwich in a brown bag and walks over to the spot where the men are eating. She walks

up to the group and with a big smile says: "Do you men know Jesus Christ?"

They shake their heads and look at each other. One of the workers looks up into the steelwork and yells, "Anybody up there know Jesus Christ?"

One of the steelworkers shouts, "Why?"

The worker yells back, "His wife's here with his lunch."

Why do men name their penis?
We don't want a total stranger making 90 per cent of our decisions.

Affordable luxury

A couple are walking down the street when the girl stops in front of a jewellery store and says, "Darling, look at that necklace! It's so beautiful."

"No problem," replies her bloke as he throws a brick through the window and grabs the sparkler.

A little later the girl points to a bracelet in the window of another shop.

"Ooh," she says. "I'd love that too!"

"No problem," says her boyfriend and, again, throws a brick through the window.

A little later they pass yet another shop when she sees a diamond ring. "Oh, honey, isn't that lovely?" she says.

"Hang about!" he says. "What do you think I am: made of bricks?"

Hail to the Chief

A man walks into a cowboy bar and orders a beer just as President Bush appears on the television.

After a few sips, he looks up at the television and mumbles, "Now, there's the biggest horse's ass I've ever seen."

A customer at the end of the bar quickly stands up, walks over to him and decks him.

"Damn it!" the man says, climbing back up to the bar. "This must be Bush country!"

"Nope," the bartender replies. "Horse country!

Cock and bull story

A London lawyer is representing a local train company in a lawsuit filed by a West Country farmer. The farmer's prize bull is missing from the section of field through which the railway passes. The farmer wants to be paid the market price for the bull and just before the case the lawyer corners the farmer and tries to get him to settle out of court. The lawyer does his best selling job and finally the farmer agrees to take half of what he was asking.

After the farmer signs the release and takes his pay-off, the young lawyer can't resist gloating a little over his success. Outside the High Court he shakes the farmer's hand and tells him, "You know, I hate to tell you this, old fella, but I put one over on you in there. I couldn't have won the case. The driver was asleep when the train went through your farm that morning. I didn't have one witness to put on the stand. I bluffed you!"

The rosy-cheeked farmer replies, "Well, I'll tell you, boy, I was a little worried about winning that case myself, because I'll be blowed if that bull didn't come home this morning."

Man of the cloth

As the congregation settles into the pews, the preacher walks to the lectern with a red face. "Some one in this congregation," he says gravely, "has spread a rumour that I belong to the Ku Klux Klan."

As a whispering spreads around the hall, the Man of God continues. "This is a horrible lie – one I am embarrassed about and one which a Christian community cannot tolerate. I ask the party who did this to stand up and ask forgiveness from God."

No one moves, so the preacher continues.

"Do you not have the nerve to face me and admit this falsehood? Remember, you will be forgiven and will feel glory in your heart."

Again all is quiet. Then, slowly, a drop-dead gorgeous blonde stands up in the third pew. "Reverend, there has been a terrible misunderstanding. I never said you were a member of the Klan."

"Oh?" says the preacher, "so what did you say?"

The blonde chews her lip and says, "I merely mentioned to a couple of friends that you were a wizard beneath the sheets."

Warm words

A doctor walks into a bank. Preparing to sign a cheque, he accidentally pulls a rectal thermometer out of his shirt pocket and tries to write with it. Realising his mistake, he looks at the thermometer with annoyance and says, "Well, that's just great. Some asshole's got my pen!"

But I thought you said...

Morris, an 82-year-old man, went to the doctor to get a physical.

A few days later, the doctor saw Morris walking down the street with a gorgeous young woman on his arm.

A couple of days later, the doctor spoke to Morris and said, "You're really doing great, aren't you?"

Morris replied, "Just doing what you said, Doc: 'Get a hot mamma and be cheerful.'"

The doctor said, "I said, 'You've got a heart murmur; be careful.'"

Blood is thicker...

Redneck Bubba's pregnant sister is in a serious car accident and she falls into a deep coma. After nearly six months she wakes up and sees that she is no longer pregnant. Frantically she asks the doctor about her baby. The doctor replies, "Ma'am, you had twins – a boy and a girl – and your babies are fine. Your brother came in and named them."

The woman thinks to herself, "Oh no! Not Bubba; he's an idiot!" Expecting the worst, she asks the doctor, "Well, what's the girl's name?"

"Denise," the doctor answers with a smile. The new mother

> What did the Native American say when the white man tied his penis in a knot?
> "How come?"

thinks, "Wow! That's a beautiful name! I guess I was wrong

about my brother. I really like the name Denise."

She then asks the doctor, "What's the boy's name?"

The doctor replies, "Denephew."

On second thoughts...

Three guys are on a trip to Saudi Arabia. One day, they stumble into a harem tent with over 100 beautiful women inside. They start getting friendly with all the women, when suddenly the Sheik storms in.

"I am the master of all these women. No one else can touch them except me. You three men must pay for what you have done today. You will be punished in a way corresponding to your profession." The Sheik turns to the first man and asks him what he does for a living.

"I'm a policeman," says the first man.

"Then we will shoot your penis off!" says the Sheik.

He then turns to the second man and asks him what he does for a living.

> **What did Keith Richards say after being inducted into the hall of fame?**
>
> 'It's a night I will remember for the rest of the night."

"I'm a fireman," says the second man.

"Then we will burn your penis off!" says the Sheik.

Finally, he asks the last man, "And you: what do you do for a living?"

And the third man answers, "I'm a lollipop salesman!"

As good as new

An Aussie lass is trying to sell her old car but she is having a lot of problems because it has almost 230,000 miles on the clock.

One day, she reveals the problem to her mate.

"There is a possibility to make the car easier to sell, but it's not legal," says her mate.

"That doesn't matter," replies the Aussie lass, "if I can only sell the car."

"OK," says her mate. "Here's the address of a friend of mine. He owns a car repair shop. Tell him I sent you and he'll 'fix it'. Then you shouldn't have a problem any more trying to sell your car."

The following weekend the Aussie lass makes the trip to the mechanic.

About one month after that, her mate asks her, "Did you sell your car?"

"No," replies the Aussie lass. "Why should I? It only has 50,000 miles on the clock."

A classic case

A man walks into a doctor's office. He has a cucumber up his nose, a carrot in his left ear and a banana in his right ear.

"What's the matter with me?" he asks the doctor.

The doctor replies, "You're not eating properly."

The smart move

A man returns home a day early from a business trip and gets into a taxi at the airport after midnight. On the way back to his house, he asks the cabby if he would be a witness as he suspects his wife is having an affair and he intends to catch her

in the act.

For £100, the cabby agrees. They arrive at the house and the husband and cabby tiptoe into the bedroom. The husband switches on the lights, yanks the blanket back and there is his wife in bed with another man.

The husband immediately puts a gun to the naked man's head.

The wife shouts, "Don't do it! This man has been very generous! I lied when I told you I inherited money. He paid for the Porsche I bought for you, your United season ticket, the house at the lake and your golf club membership and green fees."

Shaking his head from side to side the husband slowly lowers the gun and looks over at the cabbie and says, "What would you do?"

The cabby says, "I'd cover him up with that blanket before he catches a cold."

Why wasn't Jesus born in Ireland?
Because God couldn't find three wise men or a virgin.

Did you hear about the man who collected five thousand door knockers?
He won a no-bell prize.

Eternal optimist

Jake's friends always got mad at him because no matter how bad a situation was he would always say, "It could be worse."

Finally his friends decided to make up something that he couldn't say, "It could be worse" about. When they were playing golf one day Steve said to Jake, "Did you hear what happened to Fred?"

"No," said Jake.

"Fred came home Thursday and found his wife in bed with another man, killed them both and then turned the gun on himself."

"It could be worse," said Jake, predictably.

"How could it be any worse than that?" Steve asked.

"Well," Jake said, "if it had happened a day earlier, I'd be dead."

Divine protection

The new vicar's wife had a baby and he appealed to the congregation for a salary increase to cover the new addition to his family.

The congregation agreed that it was only fair and approved it.

When the next child arrived the vicar appealed and again the congregation approved the increase.

Several years and five children later, the congregation was getting hacked off with the increasing expenses. This turned into a rather loud meeting one night at the vicarage.

Finally, the vicar stood up and shouted, "Having children is an Act of God!"

An old fisherman in the back stood up and shouted back, "So are rain and snow, but we wear rubbers for them!"

Miscege-nation

On a train from London to Manchester, an American is berating the Englishman sitting across from him in the compartment.

"You English are too stiff. You set yourself apart too much. You think your stiff upper lips make you above the rest of us. Look at me; I have Italian blood, French blood, a little Indian blood and some Swedish blood. What do you say to that?"

"Very sporting of your mother," the Englishman replies.

Dog and bone

Paris Hilton, filming on location in London, rushes into a local post office. She advances to the counter, flutters her eyelashes and tells the clerk, "I just have to get an urgent message to my mom who's in America."

The clerk informs the heiress that it costs £100 if she wants it sent immediately. She replies, "But I don't have that much cash on me and I must get a message to her straightaway; it's soooo urgent! I'll do anything to get a message to her."

"Anything?" the young clerk asks.

"Yes, anything!" replies the blonde.

He leads her back to the office and closes the door. He tells

her to kneel in front of him and unzip his trousers. She does. "Take it out," he says. She does this as well.

She looks up at him, his manhood in her hands, and he says, "Well… what are you waiting for? Go ahead and do it."

Paris brings her lips close to it and shouts, "Hello? Mom?"

Prize ass

A redneck, named Kenny, buys a donkey from a farmer for £100. The farmer agrees to deliver the donkey the next day.

The next day the farmer drives up and says, "Sorry, son, but I have some bad news; the donkey's dead."

Kenny replies, "Well, then, just give me my money back."

The farmer says, "I can't do that. I went and spent it already."

Kenny says, "OK, then; just bring me the dead donkey."

The farmer asks, "What are you going to do with him?"

Kenny says, "I'm going to raffle him off."

A month later, the farmer meets up with Kenny and asks, "What happened with that dead donkey?"

Kenny says, "I raffled him off, like I said I was going to. I sold 500 tickets at two pounds a piece and made a profit of £998."

The farmer says, "Didn't anyone complain?"

Kenny says, "Just the guy who won: so I gave him his two pound back."

Hippocratic oaf

A drunk goes to the doctor complaining of tiredness and headaches. "I feel tired all the time," he slurs. "My head hurts and I'm not sleeping. What is it, Doc?"

Frowning, the doctor examines him before standing back. "I

can't find anything wrong," he says. "It must be the drinking."

"Fair enough," replies the lush. "I'll come back when you sober up."

Natural selection

Four men are bragging about how smart their cats are. The first man is an engineer, the second man is an accountant, the third a chemist and the fourth man is a mechanic.

To show off, the engineer calls his cat: "T-square, do your stuff." T-square prances over to the desk, takes out some paper and pen and promptly draws a circle, a square and a triangle. Everyone agrees that he's pretty smart.

However, the accountant thinks his cat can do better. He calls his cat: "Spreadsheet, do your stuff." Spreadsheet goes out to the kitchen and returns with a dozen biscuits. He divides them into four equal piles of three biscuits. Everyone agrees that he's good.

But the chemist says his cat can do better. He calls his cat: "Measure, do your stuff." Measure gets up, walks to the

---

Why was the leper caught speeding?
He couldn't take his foot of the accelerator.

---

fridge, takes out a pint of milk, gets a 10-ounce glass from the cupboard and pours exactly eight ounces without spilling a drop. Everyone agrees that he's pretty good.

Then the three men turn to the mechanic and ask: "What can your cat do?" The mechanic calls his cat: "Coffee Break, do your stuff." Coffee Break jumps to his feet, eats the biscuits,

drinks the milk, craps on the paper, screws the other three cats, claims he injured his back while doing so, files a report for unsafe working conditions and goes home for the rest of the day on sick leave.

Got you there

A married man goes to confession and says to his priest, "I almost had an affair with another woman."

The priest replies, "Almost?" The man says, "Well, we got undressed and rubbed together; I stopped."

"Rubbing together is the same as putting it in! Say five Hail Marys and put £50 in the poor box."

The man leaves and pauses by the poor box. The watching priest runs over to him saying, "I saw that. You didn't put any money in the poor box!"

The man replies, "Yeah, but I rubbed the £50 on it and, according to you, that's the same as putting it in."

Ball skills

A boy walks into a sports shop and tells the staff that he has an amazing talent; he can tell which club emblem any football has printed on it just by feeling it. So the staff blindfold the young lad and hand him a ball.

He feels it and says, "Blackpool. I can smell the sea and feel the sand."

The amazed staff hand him another. He feels it and says, "It's Partick Thistle, I can smell the heather and feel the thistles."

Then they hand him another and he instantly says, "West Ham." One of the members of staff is amazed, "How did you get that one so quickly?"

"It's going down," the boy replies.

Buns for tea

A baker hires a young female assistant who likes to wear very short skirts and a thong. One day a young man enters the store, glances at the assistant and glances at the loaves of bread behind the counter. Noticing the length of her skirt and the location of the raisin bread, he has a brilliant idea.

"I'd like some raisin bread, please," the man says politely. The girl nods and climbs up a ladder to reach the raisin bread, which is located on the very top shelf. The young man, standing almost directly beneath her, gets an excellent view just as he planned. Once she comes down, he says he should get two loaves, as he's having company for dinner.

As the girl retrieves the second loaf of bread, one of the other male customers notices what's going on. Thinking quickly, he requests his own loaf of raisin bread so he can continue to enjoy the view.

With each trip up the ladder, the young lady seems to catch the eye of another male customer. Pretty soon, each male customer is asking for raisin bread, just to see her climb up and down. After many trips she's tired, irritated and thinking that she's really going to have to try the bread herself.

Finally, once again atop the ladder, she stops and fumes, glaring at the men standing below. She notices an elderly man standing among the crowd, staring up at her. Thinking to save herself a trip, she yells at the old man, "Is it raisin for you, too?"

"No," stammers the old man, "but it's quivering a bit!"

Damned if you do...

A girl is waiting to enter Heaven when she hears horrible screams of pain and torture coming from inside. She says to St. Peter, "What's going on?" He says, "That's the sound of new angels getting big holes drilled into their backs for their wings, and small holes drilled into their heads for their halos."

She says, "Heaven sounds terrible. I think maybe I'd rather go to Hell."

St. Peter says, "But down there it's hot, smelly and you have to fornicate with anything that moves."

She says, "That's OK; I've already got the holes for that."

Short, sharp shock

Two young guys are picked up by the cops for being drunk and disorderly, and appear in court before the judge. The judge tells them, "You seem like nice young men and I'd like to give you a second chance rather than jail time. I want you to go out this weekend and show others the evils of binge-drinking and get them to give up the booze for ever. I'll see you back in court on Monday."

When the two guys return to court, the judge asks the first one, "So, how did you do over the weekend?"

"Well, Your Honour, I managed to persuade 17 people to give up booze for ever."

"Seventeen people!" says the judge. "That's wonderful. What did you tell them?"

"I used a diagram, Your Honour. I drew a big circle and a small circle and told them that the big circle is your brain without booze and the small circle is your brain after a session."

"That's admirable," says the judge, turning to the second guy. "And you, how did you do?"

"Well, Your Honour, I managed to persuade 156 people to give up alcohol for ever."

"One hundred and fifty-six people? That's incredible! How did you manage to do that?"

"Well, I used the same diagram, only I pointed to the small circle first and said, 'This is your asshole before prison...'"

Down, boy

A man takes his cross-eyed dog to the vet. The vet picks him up and examines him for a while and then says, "I'm going to have to put this dog down."

"What? Because he's cross-eyed?"

"No: because he's getting heavy."

Time and punishment

The cops are ordered to clean up the High Street for a big parade and are patrolling the pavements when a drunk staggers towards them. "Excuse me, offisher," he says to one constable, "could you pleash tell me the time?"

The constable frowns at him. "One o'clock," he says, before whacking him once over the head with his truncheon.

"Christ!" says the drunk, reeling. "I'm glad I didn't ask you an hour ago!"

Curry On Doctor

With a screech of brakes, an ambulance pulls up at the local casualty ward and a hippie is wheeled out on a hospital trolley. The doctor questions the man's hippie friends about his situation.

"So what was he doing then?" asks the physician. "Acid? Cannabis?"

"Sort of," replies one of the hippies, nervously thumbing his kaftan, "but we ran out of gear, so I skinned up a home-made spliff."

"And what was in that?" asks the doctor.

"Um… I kind of raided my girlfriend's spice rack," says the hippie. "There was a bit of cumin, some turmeric and a little paprika."

"Well, that explains it," the doctor replies, looking at them gravely. "He's in a korma."

What does Ashley Giles put in his hands to make sure the next ball almost always takes a wicket?
A bat.

Once bitten...

A guy walks into a bar with his pet monkey. He orders a drink and the monkey runs around before grabbing some olives off the bar and eating them. Next he eats the sliced lime before he jumps up on the pool table, grabs the cue ball and swallows it whole.

The barman yells, "Did you see what your monkey just did?"

"No, what?" replies the man.

"He just ate the cue ball off my pool table – whole!"

"Yeah, that doesn't surprise me," replies the patron. "He eats everything in sight, the little twerp. I'll pay for the cue ball and stuff." He finishes his drink, pays his bill and leaves.

Two weeks later he returns with his monkey. He orders a drink and the monkey starts running around the bar again.

While the man is drinking, the monkey finds a maraschino cherry on the bar. He sticks it up his butt, pulls it out, and eats it. The bartender is disgusted. "Did you see what your monkey did now?"

"What?" asks the riled drinker.

"He stuck a maraschino cherry up his bottom, then pulled it out and ate it!"

"Yeah, that doesn't surprise me either," replies the man. "He still eats everything in sight, but ever since he ate that damn cue ball he measures everything first!"

Top marks for thinking

Little Johnny is in a class where every Friday the teacher asks a question and if you get it right you don't have to go to school on Monday.

The first Friday the question is, "How many gallons of water are there in the whole world?"

No one knows so they all have to go to school on Monday.

Next Friday, the question is, "How many grains of sand are there in the whole world?"

Again, the class is clueless so they have to go to school on Monday.

Now Little Johnny is getting angry because he doesn't want to go to school on Monday, so he paints two ping-pong balls black.

The next Friday right before the teacher asks her weekly question Johnny rolls the two balls up to her.

Angrily, the teacher asks, "Ok, who's the comedian with two black balls?"

Little Johnny replies: "Chris Rock. See you Tuesday!"

Top of the plops

Two flies land on a steaming heap of manure.

The first lifts his leg and farts.

The other fly says, "Jesus, Jim, I'm trying to eat."

Bogged down

During training exercises, a British Army lieutenant is driving down a muddy back road and encounters another jeep stuck in the mud with a red-faced colonel at the wheel.

"Your jeep stuck, sir?" asks the lieutenant as he pulled alongside.

"Nope," replies the colonel, coming over and handing him the keys,

"Yours is."

Ewe get yer own!

An Australian is on holiday in New Zealand and is walking through a farm when he comes across a New Zealander having sex with a sheep.

The Australian says to the New Zealander, "In Australia we shear them."

The New Zealander looks horrified. "I'm not shearing this with nobody!"

Eve of destruction

In the beginning, God created the earth and rested.

Then God created Man and rested.

Then God created Woman.

Since then, neither God nor Man has rested.

Figure of fun

On his first night in prison, a convict is glumly eating his dinner when another inmate jumps to his feet, shouts, "Thirty-seven!" and all the other inmates laugh hysterically. Another shouts back, "Four hundred and twenty!" and gets the same reaction.

"What's going on?" says the new inmate to his cellmate.

"It's like this," says the convict. "We only have one joke book in this prison and everyone knows all the jokes off by heart, so instead of telling the whole joke, we just stand up and shout out a page number."

A few days later, the new convict decides that it's time to join in, so he stands up and shouts, "Fourteen!"

Total silence ensues. Turning to his cellmate, he asks, "What went wrong?"

The convict replies, "It's the way you tell 'em."

How do you know if you've caught bird flu?
You're suddenly unable to park and all you can talk about is shoes.

From here to maternity

What did the Aussie lass say to the doctor when she got pregnant?

Are you sure it's mine?

The Great and Powerful

Former Presidents Bill Clinton and George Bush Snr are travelling through Kansas with George Bush Jnr.

A tornado comes along and whirls them up into the air and tosses them thousands of miles away. They all fall into a daze. When they come to and stumble out of the limousine, they realise they're in the fabled Land of Oz.

They decide to go to see the famous Wizard of Oz, known for granting people their wishes.

Bush Jnr says, "I'm going to ask the Wizard for a brain."

Bush Snr responds, "I'm going to ask the Wizard for a heart."

Clinton thinks for a moment, and says, "Where's Dorothy?"

Local knowledge

A Scotsman, an Englishman and an Aussie are having a drink in America.

"Y'know," says the Scotsman, "I still prefer the pubs back home. In Glasgow there's a little bar called McTavish's. Now the landlord there goes out of his way for the locals so much that when you buy four drinks, he'll buy the fifth one for you."

"Well," says the Englishman, "at my local, the Red Lion, the barman there will buy you your third drink after you buy the first two."

"Ahhhhh, that's nothing," says the Aussie. "Back home in Sydney there's Bruce's Bar. Now, the moment you set foot in the place they'll buy you a drink, then another, all the drinks you like. Then, when you've had enough drinks, they'll take you upstairs and see that you get laid, and it's all on the house."

The Englishman and Scotsman immediately scorn the Aussie's claims. But the Aussie swears every word is true.

"Well," says the Englishman, "has this actually happened to you?"

"Not me personally, no," says the Aussie. "But it did happen to my sister."

Bungle in the jungle

Alan Curbishley goes on a scouting mission to the South American rainforest. When he arrives he spots a huge local tribesman standing in a clearing. Suddenly a huge seedpod drops from a tree and the man volleys it with incredible power and precision through a tiny hole in the foliage.

"Bloody hell!" says Curbs. "Can you do that again?"

So the tribesman does exactly the same thing, only this time he juggles the pod from foot to foot before blasting it through the hole in the foliage.

Needless to say, Curbishley signs up the tribesman from the rainforest and proudly shows him off at the next West Ham training session.

"Before we go any further," says Curbs, "ball" (pointing at the ball); "goal" (pointing at the goal). "That's Ball and Goal."

"But, boss," protests the tribesman, "I can speak perfect English."

"I know that," replies the desperate manager, "I was talking to the rest of the team."

Slow food

Three tourists were driving through Wales. As they were
approaching Llanfairpwllgwyngyllgogerchwyrndrobwllllanty-
siliogogogoch, they started arguing about the pronunciation
of the town's name. They argued back and forth until they

> **What do you get after five days of non-stop sex?**
> **A weak end.**

stopped for lunch.

As they stood at the counter one asked the blonde
employee, "Before we order, could you please settle an
argument for us? Would you please pronounce where we
are... very slowly?"

The girl leaned over the counter and said, "Burrrrrrgerrrrrr
Kiiiiiing."

Stupid bankers

Roman Abramovich walks into a bank in London and asks to
see the manager. "I'm going to Moscow on business for two
weeks and need to borrow £5,000," says Roman.

The manager replies, "I'm afraid we'll still need some kind of
security for the loan."

"No problem," says the Blues' boss and hands over the keys
to his brand new Bentley.

The bank agrees to accept the car as collateral for the loan
and the manager and the tellers all enjoy a good laugh at the
Russian's expense for using a £200,000 car as collateral against

**What will history remember Bill Clinton as?
The President after Bush.**

a £5,000 loan. An employee of the bank then proceeds to drive the Bentley into the bank's underground garage and parks it there. Two weeks later, Roman returns, repays the £5,000 and interest, which comes to £15.41.

The manager says, "We are very happy to have had your business, Mr Abramovich, and this transaction has worked out very nicely, but we are a little puzzled. Why would you bother to borrow £5,000? You're one of the richest men in the world."

Roman replies, "Where else in London can I park my car for two weeks for only £15.41 and expect it to be there when I return?"

Without a prayer

One night before bed, Arsène Wenger is trying to think of ways to get Arsenal's season back on track. As a last resort, he prays to God. God hears his prayers and decides to take pity on him. Later that night, Wenger suddenly awakes to see the Lord in front of him.

"Come forth, my son!" says the Lord.

To which Wenger replies, "Fourth? We'll be lucky if we finish bloody fifth."

Full of clap

Bono's fronting the home leg of U2's latest world tour in Dublin when he asks the audience for some quiet. Then he starts to slowly clap his hands and, as he does so, says into the microphone, "Every time I clap my hands, a child in Africa dies."

A voice from near the front pierces the silence: "Well, stop f**king clapping, then!"

Encountering turbulence

A guy sitting at a bar at Heathrow notices an attractive woman sitting next to him. He thinks to himself: "Wow, she's so gorgeous she must be a flight attendant. But which airline does she work for?"

Hoping to pick her up, he leans towards her and utters the Delta Airways slogan: "Love to fly and it shows?"

She gives him a blank, confused stare.

A moment later, the Singapore Airlines slogan pops into his head. He leans towards her again, "Something special in the air?"

She gives him the same confused look.

Next he tries the Thai Airways slogan: "Smooth as silk."

This time the woman turns to him and says, "What the fuck do you want?"

The man smiles, slumps back in his chair, and says "Ahhhhh: Air New Zealand!"

Beach bombs

Two seagulls were flying over the beach at a seaside resort one boiling hot August Bank Holiday afternoon. Every way they looked, there were so many people there wasn't a speck of sand to be seen.

"Ah," said one to the other contemptuously, "takes all the skill out of it, doesn't it?"

When push comes to shove

After hearing a couple's complaints that their sex life isn't what it used to be, the sex counsellor suggests they vary their position.

"For example," he says, "you might try the wheelbarrow. Lift her legs from behind and off you go."

The eager husband is all for trying this new idea as soon as they get home.

"Well, OK," the hesitant wife agrees, "but on two conditions. First, if it hurts you have to stop right away, and second you have to promise we won't go past my parents' house."

Dream come true

Three blokes, an Englishman, a Frenchman and a Welshman, are out walking along the beach. They come across a lantern and a genie pops out of it. "I will give you each one wish!" cries the genie.

The Welshman says, "I'm a farmer, my dad was a farmer, and my son will also farm. I want the land to be forever fertile in Wales."

With a blink of the genie's eye, 'FOOM' – the land in Wales

What does Britney say after sex?
"Are you boys all in the same band?"

is forever made fertile for farming.

The Frenchman is amazed, "I want a wall around France, so that no one can invade our precious country," he says.

Again, with a blink of the Genie's eye, 'FOOM' – there is a huge wall around France.

The Englishman asks, "I'm very curious. Please tell me more about this wall."

The Genie explains, "Well, it's about 150 feet high, 50 feet thick and nothing can get in or out."

The Englishman says, "Fill it up with water."

Gotcha!

Two Aussies, Wayne and Shayne, go camping. They pack a cooler with sandwiches and beer and set off. After two days of hiking, they arrive at a great spot but soon realise that they've forgotten to pack a bottle opener.

Wayne turns to Shayne and says, "You gotta go back and get the opener or else we have no beer."

"No way, mate," says Shayne. "By the time I get back, you'll have eaten all the food."

"I promise I won't," says Wayne. "Just hurry!"

Five full days pass and there's still no sign of Shayne. Exasperated and starving, Wayne gives in to hunger and digs into the sandwiches. Suddenly, Shayne pops out from behind a rock and yells, "I knew it! I'm not f**king going!"

Doctor, Doctor

One night, a man and a woman are at a bar downing a few beers. They strike up a conversation and quickly discover that they're both doctors. After about an hour, the man says to the woman, "Hey, how about we sleep together tonight?

No strings attached. It'll just be one night of fun."

The woman agrees. So they go back to her place. She goes into the bathroom and starts scrubbing up like she's about to go into the operating room.

She scrubs for a good 10-20 minutes. Finally, she goes into the bedroom and they have sex for an hour or so. Afterwards, the man says to the woman, "You're a surgeon, aren't you?"

"Yeah, how did you know?" she replies.

"I could tell by the way you scrubbed up before we started," he says.

"Oh, that makes sense," says the woman.

"You're an anaesthetist, aren't you?"

"Yeah," says the man, a bit taken aback. "How did you know?"

The woman answers, "I didn't feel a thing!"

Increasing frustration

The Hunchback of Notre Dame returns home from a hard day's ringing the cathedral bells and finds his beautiful wife standing in the kitchen holding a wok.

"Fantastic, Esmeralda," says the Hunchback, "I really fancy some Chinese food."

"Oh, no, not tonight, Quasi," she says, "I'm ironing your shirts."

Beastly behaviour

A gorilla and a rhino are best mates until one day, as the rhino bends over to drink at the watering hole, the gorilla takes advantage of the situation and jumps him from behind. The rhino is furious and chases the gorilla all over the savannah. Half an hour later, still being chased by the rhino, the gorilla spots a tourist sitting in a chair, reading

a newspaper. Quick as a flash, he knocks the tourist unconscious, strips him, hides him in the bush, puts on his clothes and sits down in his chair. Moments later, the rhino comes charging past and asks:

"Have you seen a gorilla around here anywhere?"

Holding the paper up to hide his face, the gorilla replies: "What, the one that rogered the rhino by the watering hole?"

"Oh, shit," says the rhino, "don't tell me it's in the papers already."

Toad in the hole

Walking down the high street, a woman spies a shop doorway she's never seen before. Pinned to the front is a sign: "Lady-pleasing frog – inside."

Checking to make sure no one's watching, she darts in – only to find an almost bare room. "Er, can you help me?" she asks the man behind the counter. He looks up and grins widely, "Oui, mademoiselle!"

We'll cashew one day...

An elderly couple had a parlour in which they kept a couple of food bins. One of those bins contained apples and the other bin contained nuts. They were having quite a bit of trouble with mice, so one evening before going to bed they set a couple of mouse traps, one by the bin of apples and one by the bin of nuts. During the night they heard a trap snap. The old gentleman got up to see which mouse trap had caught a mouse.

On returning to bed his wife asked, "Well, did we catch him by the apples?"

The old gentleman replied, "Nope. Try again."

Natural disaster

How are tornadoes and marriage alike?

They both begin with a lot of blowing and sucking, and in the end you lose your house.

Accident victim

A woman and a man driver are involved in a horrific collision, but amazingly both escape unhurt – though their cars are written off.

As they crawl out of the wreckage, the man sees the woman is blonde and strikingly beautiful. Then the woman turns to the man and gushes: "That's incredible, our cars are demolished but we're fine. It's a sign from God that we're meant to be together!"

Sensing a promise, the man stammers, "Yes, I agree!"

The woman continues, "And look; though my car was destroyed, this bottle of wine survived! It must be another sign. Let's drink to our love!"

"OK!" says the man, going with the moment. She offers him the bottle, he downs half of it and hands it back.

"Your turn," says the man.

"No, thanks," she replies, "I think I'll just wait for the police."

What's the difference between kinky and perverted?
Kinky is using the feather; perverted is using the chicken.

See you later, applicator

Two young boys go into a pharmacy, pick up a box of Tampax and walk to the counter. "How old are you, son?" enquires the pharmacist. "Eight."

"Do you know how these are used?" "Not exactly," says the boy, "but they aren't for me. They're for my brother; he's four. We saw on TV that if you use these you'll be able to swim and ride a bike, and he can't do either."

For I have sinned

A drunken man staggers into a Catholic church, sits down in the confessional and says nothing. The bewildered priest coughs to attract his attention, but still the man says nothing.

The priest then knocks on the wall three times in a final attempt to get the man to confess. Finally, the drunk replies, "No use knockin', mate; there's no paper in this one either."

Skin game

A man is working at the zoo when his boss says, "The gorilla is sick today and it's the busiest day of the year – you'll have to put on this gorilla suit so as not to disappoint the public."

"No chance," says the man. However, his boss warns him that if he doesn't put on the suit and pretend to be the gorilla he'll be sacked. Grudgingly, the man gets dressed and jumps into the gorilla's cage. After a while he starts to enjoy it and begins showing off. Without warning, his tyre swing snaps and he lands in the lion's den. The male lion pounces on him and starts mauling the man, who begins screaming for his life. Suddenly he hears the lion say, "Shut up or we'll both get the sack!"

Beyond a choke

A man walks through a big shopping centre with his teenage son.

The boy tosses a 50p up in the air and catches it between his teeth to impress his dad, but he fails to clamp down with his teeth and ends up choking on the money. As the boy coughs and wheezes the father panics and shouts, "Help! Is there a doctor in the house? My son's choking!"

Not too far from the action, a man sitting in a cafe reading a paper hears the father's cries and patiently puts down his coffee and folds his paper. He then walks over to the boy, grabs him by the balls and squeezes the hell out of them.

The startled lad immediately coughs up the 50p and the man catches it in his hand and walks away.

The amazed father runs over and says, "Thank you, sir; you saved my son's life. Are you a doctor?"

"No," the man replies, "I work for HM Revenue and Customs."

Hairy moment

A man walks into a restaurant and orders a cheeseburger.

Later, the waitress brings his meal to him. He takes a bite out of it and notices there's a small hair in the hamburger. He begins yelling frantically at the waitress, "Waitress, there's a hair in my hamburger! I demand to see what's going on!"

So the waitress takes him to the kitchen and, to his horror, he sees the cook take the meat patty and flatten it under his armpit. He says, "That's disgusting!"

The waitress replies, "You think that's disgusting? You should see him make doughnuts."

Hear, hear

Sadly, Dave was born without ears, and though he proved to be successful in business, his problem annoyed him greatly.

One day he needed to hire a new manager for his company, so he set up three interviews. The first man was great. He knew everything he needed to know and was very interesting. But at the end of the interview, Dave asked him, "Do you notice anything different about me?"

"Why, yes; I couldn't help but notice that you have no ears," came the reply. Dave didn't appreciate his honesty and threw him out of the office.

> **Why is getting up at three in the morning like a pig's tail?**
> **It's twirly.**

The second interview was with a woman and she was even better.

But he asked her the same question: "Do you notice anything different about me?"

"Well," she said, stammering, "you have no ears."

Dave again got upset and chucked her out in a rage.

The third and final interviewee, a young student, was the best of the bunch.

Dave was anxious, but went ahead and asked the young man the same question: "Do you notice anything different about me?"

Much to Dave's surprise, the young man answered, "Yes; you

wear contact lenses, don't you?"

Dave was shocked. He'd finally found the perfect person for the job.

"How in the world did you know that?" he asked delighted.

The young man fell off his chair, laughing hysterically, and replied, "Well, it's pretty hard to wear glasses with no bloody ears!"

Reversal of fortune

A man goes into a bar and sees a friend at a table, drinking by himself.

"You look terrible," says the man. "What's the problem?"

"My mother died in August," says the friend, "and left me £25,000."

"Gee, that's tough," replies the man.

"Then in September," the friend continues, staring deep into his glass, "my father died, leaving me £90,000."

"Wow! Two parents gone in two months. No wonder you're depressed."

"And last month my aunt died, and left me £15,000."

"Three close family members lost in three months. How sad," says the man in a comforting tone.

"Then this month," his friend goes on, "absolutely nothing!"

Heated debate

A man is in a butcher's in Glasgow. The butcher is out the back, by a radiator. The man is looking at the counter and shouts, "Is that your Ayrshire bacon?"

The butcher shouts back, "No, I'm just warming my hands."

Teed off

A golfer is about to tee off when he's approached by a man holding out a card that reads, "I am a deaf mute. May I please play through?"

The guy gives the card back, angrily shaking his head. Assuming the guy can lip-read, he adds, "I can't believe you would try to use your handicap for a cheap advantage like that! Of course you can't play through!"

The deaf man walks away and the guy whacks the ball on to the green and then walks off to finish the hole.

Just as the golfer is about to putt out, he's hit in the head with a golf ball that knocks him out cold.

When he comes to a few minutes later, he looks around and sees the deaf mute sternly looking at him, one hand on his driver, the other hand holding up four fingers.

What is the similarity between PlayStations and breasts?
Both are made for children, but used by adults.

All mod cons

A salesman checks into a futuristic hotel. Needing a haircut before his meeting, he calls reception to see if there's a barber on the premises.

"I'm afraid not, sir," the receptionist tells him, "but down the hall from your room is a vending machine that should serve your purposes."

Sceptical but intrigued, the salesman locates the machine, inserts £10 and sticks his head into the opening, at which point the machine starts to buzz and spin. Fifteen seconds later, he pulls out his head and looks in the mirror to see the best haircut of his life.

"That's amazing," he says before noticing another machine with a sign reading, "For 50p this machine will provide a service men need when away from their wives…" Very excited, he skips the rest of the description and puts the coin in the slot.

"Oh, man. Do I ever need this!" he gasps, looking both ways and unzipping his fly. When the machine starts buzzing, he lets out a shriek of agony and almost passes out. Fifteen seconds later, it shuts off. With trembling hands, the man withdraws his member, which now has a button neatly sewn on the end.

First the bad news...

In the middle of poker night John loses a £500 hand, clutches his chest and drops dead on the floor. His mate Pete is designated as the guy who has to go and give his wife the bad news.

"Be gentle with her, Pete," one of the other players says. "They were childhood sweethearts."

So Pete walks over to John's house, knocks on the door, and tries his best to be helpful. "Your husband just lost £500 playing cards."

"Tell that idiot to drop dead," shouts the wife.

"I'll tell him," Pete says.

Holy matrimony

On their way to get married, a young couple are involved in a fatal car accident. The couple find themselves sitting outside the Pearly Gates waiting for St. Peter to process them into Heaven. While waiting, they begin to wonder; could they possibly get married in Heaven? When St. Peter shows up, they ask him.

St. Peter says, "I don't know. This is the first time anyone has asked. Let me go and find out."

He goes off to get to the bottom of it. The couple sit down to wait for an answer... for a couple of months. St. Peter finally returns looking somewhat bedraggled.

"Yes," he informs the couple, "you can get married in Heaven."

"Great!" says the couple, "But we were just wondering, what if things don't work out? Could we also get a divorce in Heaven?"

St. Peter, red-faced with anger, slams his clipboard on to the ground.

"What's wrong?" ask the frightened couple.

"Come on!" St. Peter shouts. "It took me two months to find a priest up here! Do you have any idea how long it'll take me to find a lawyer?"

Tooled up

After years of stuttering, Jim finally goes to the doctor to see
if he can be cured. The doctor thoroughly examines him, and
asks him to drop his pants – whereupon Jim's massive member
thuds on to the table. "Hmm," says the physician. "I see the
problem – because of gravity your penis's weight is putting too
much strain on the vocal chords in your neck."

"B-b-b-ut wh-wh-at c-c-c-an b-b-be d-done?" asks Jim.

The doctor smiles. "Don't worry. Modern surgery can work
miracles. We can replace your penis with one of normal size
and the stuttering will instantly disappear."

Convinced, Jim agrees to the op – and as the doctor
promised, his stuttering completely stops afterwards. About
three months later, however, he returns to the doctor's surgery.
"Doc, I'm still grateful for what you did," he says, "but my wife
really misses the size of my old member. So I've decided I'll live
with stuttering for the rest of my life, and get my old dick back."

The doctor shakes his head, sadly. "Hey," he says, "a d-d-de-
deal's a d-d-deal."

What's the difference between a conference
footballer and a KFC bucket?
The KFC can feed a family of four.

Land of my Godfathers

Did you hear about the Welsh Mafia boss?

He'll make you an offer you can't understand.

Paradise island

A retired corporate executive decides to take a holiday. He books himself on a Caribbean cruise and proceeds to have the time of his life – that is, until the ship sinks. He finds himself on an island with no other people, no supplies, nothing. After about four months, he is lying on the beach when the most gorgeous woman he has ever seen rows up to the shore.

In disbelief, he asks, "Where did you come from? How did you get here?"

She replies, "I rowed from the other side of the island. I landed here when my cruise ship sank."

"Amazing," he notes. "You were really lucky to have a row boat wash up with you."

"Oh, this thing?" explains the woman. "I made the boat out of raw material I found on the island. The oars were whittled from gum tree branches. I wove the bottom from palm branches, and the sides and stern came from a eucalyptus tree."

"But, where did you get the tools?" asks the amazed castaway.

"Oh, that was no problem," replies the woman. "On the south side of the island, a very unusual stratum of alluvial rock is exposed. I found if I fired it to a certain temperature in my kiln, it melted like iron. I used that for tools and used the tools to make the hardware." The guy is stunned.

"Let's row over to my place," she says. After a few minutes of rowing, she docks the boat at a small wharf. As the man looks

to shore, he nearly falls off the boat. Before him is a stone walk leading to an exquisite bungalow painted in blue and white. Trying to hide his continuing amazement, the man accepts a drink and they sit down on her sofa to talk.

"I'm going to slip into something more comfortable," says the woman. She soon returns wearing nothing but vines, strategically positioned. She beckons for him to sit down next to her.

"Tell me," she begins suggestively, "We've been out here for many months. You've been lonely. There's something I'm sure you've been longing for…" She stares into his eyes.

He can't believe what he's hearing. "You mean," he swallows excitedly and tears start to well in his eyes, "you've built a kebab shop?"

In-car entertainment

A man buys a new car, but returns the next day, complaining that he can't figure out how the radio works. The salesman explains that the radio is voice-activated.

"Watch this!" he says… "Beatles!"

Sure enough, 'Eleanor Rigby' starts blaring from the speakers.

The man drives away happy and, for the next few days, every time he says a band's name he gets their greatest hits.

One day, a dangerous driver runs a red light and nearly creams his high-tech car, but he swerves in time to avoid the man, who yells, "Assholes!" All of a sudden the German national anthem, sung by Coldplay, comes on the radio…

What's another name for push-up bras?
False advertising.

Law of nature

A female TV reporter arranges for an interview with a farmer, seeking the main cause of Mad Cow disease. "Good evening, sir. I am here to collect information on possible causes of Mad Cow Disease. Can you offer any reason for this disease?" she asks.

The farmer stares at the reporter. "Do you know that a bull mounts a cow only once a year?" he asks.

The embarrassed reporter replies: "Well, sir, that's a new piece of information, but what's the relation between this phenomenon and Mad Cow disease?"

"And, madam, do you know that we milk a cow twice a day?" he asks, ignoring her.

"Sir, this is really valuable information, but what about getting to the point?" she retorts.

"I am getting to the point, madam. Just imagine; if I was playing with your breasts twice a day and only having sex with you once a year, wouldn't you get mad?"

What will you get if Man United are relegated this season?
About 70,000 more Chelsea fans.

Monstrous regiment

Why is getting a new girlfriend like joining the army?

You're forced to have a new haircut, a new set of clothes, and you only get information on a need-to-know basis.

The shellfish gene

One day, in the shark-infested waters of the Carribean, two prawns called Justin and Christian are discussing the pressures of being a preyed-upon prawn.

"I hate being a prawn," says Justin "I wish I were a shark."

Suddenly a mysterious cod appears. "Your wish is granted," he says.

Instantly Justin becomes a shark. Horrified, Christian swims away, afraid his former friend might eat him. As time passes, Christian continues to avoid Justin, leaving the shrimp-turned-predator lonely and frustrated. So when he bumps into the cod again, he begs the mysterious fish to change him back. Lo and behold, Justin is turned back into a prawn. With tears of joy in his tiny little eyes, he swims back to the reef to seek out Christian.

As he approaches, he shouts out: "It's me, Justin, your old friend. I've changed... I've found Cod. I'm a prawn again, Christian."

Second opinion

An old fella with a dodgy heart goes to see his doctor about some chest pains he's been experiencing.

When he gets home his wife asks him if he's been prescribed medication. "No, nothing like that," says the old man. "I'm going to make some lunch."

Wanting to give him some space, the wife lets her husband go. Ten minutes later she hears screams of pain coming from the kitchen and rushes in to find the old guy cooking a fry-up in a biscuit tin and burning his fingers whenever he touches it.

"What on earth are you doing?" she screams.

"Just following doctor's orders," says the old man. "He said the best thing I can do for my heart is to throw away the frying pan."

Slip-up

A boy comes home from school looking sheepish. "Dad," he moans, "we had a class spelling contest today and I failed on the very first word."

"Ah, that's OK, son," says his father, looking over his glasses at him. "What was the word?"

The son looks miserable. "Posse," he replies.

His father bursts out laughing. "Well, no wonder you couldn't spell it," he roars. "You can't even pronounce it."

> **What do you call a man with no arms or legs playing the piano?**
> **A clever dick.**

Stripped for action

A soldier at the Pentagon gets out of the shower and realises that his clothes are missing. He searches around for them, but accidentally locks himself out of his locker room, and finds himself completely naked in the halls of the HQ of the world's most powerful military organization. But, luckily, no one is around to see him.

So he runs as fast as he can to the elevator. When it arrives, it's empty. He breathes a sigh of relief and gets in. When the doors open on his floor, there is no one waiting outside. "This must be my lucky day," he says to himself. He is now only a few yards from his office.

Suddenly, he hears footsteps coming from around the corner. He hears the General's voice. There is no way he'll make it to his door in time, so he ducks into the closest office available, and finds himself in the laboratory for Research & Development. The Head Scientist looks up from one of her experiments with puzzled interest.

The soldier thinks quickly, stands up straight and salutes.

"I am here to report the partial success of the Personal Invisibility Device," he says.

"I see," the Head Scientist says. "The Shrink Ray seems to be working perfectly, though."

The truth hurts

Tired of a listless sex life, a husband asks his wife during lovemaking, "How come you never tell me when you have an orgasm?"

To which she replies, "You're never here!"

Bliss eternal

Two brothers, Brian and Phil, make a deal that whichever one dies first will contact the living one from the afterlife. Brian dies a few years later. Phil doesn't hear from him for about a year and ruefully figures that there is no afterlife.

Then one day he gets a call. It's Brian. "So there is an afterlife! What's it like?" asks Phil.

"Well," begins Brian. "I sleep really late. I get up, have a big breakfast, then I have sex – lots of sex. Then I go back to sleep, but I get up for lunch, have a big lunch and have some more sex – lots more sex. Then I take a nap. Then a huge dinner and loads more sex. Then I go to sleep and wake up the next day."

"Oh, my God," says Phil. "Heaven sounds amazing!"

"I'm not in heaven," says Brian. "I'm a lion in Windsor Safari Park."

Sheer brass neck

Every day, Tony Blair jogs past a prostitute who stands on the same street corner near the Houses of Parliament. "Two hundred and fifty quid for you, Tony!" she shouts from the kerb.

Embarrassed, the ex-Prime Minister feels he has to shout something just to shut her up, so he yells: "No! A fiver!"

This ritual soon becomes a daily occurrence.

One day, Cherie Blair decides that she wants to accompany her husband on his daily jog. As the couple nears the working woman's street corner, Tony realises she will bark her £250 offer and Mrs B will wonder what he's really been doing on all his past outings.

As the pair jogs into the turn that takes them past the corner, the premier becomes even more apprehensive than usual.

Sure enough, there is the prostitute. Tony tries to avoid

her eyes as she watches the pair jog past but, amazingly, she doesn't say anything. Tony can't believe his luck. Then suddenly from her corner, the hooker yells after them, "See what you get for a fiver?"

Why can't you circumcise a Morris dancer?
Because they have to be complete dicks.

Mucky ducky

A woman is taking a stroll through the woods when a little white duck, covered in filth, crosses her path.

"Let me clean you," the woman says, taking a tissue from her bag.

The woman walks on a little further and encounters another duck, also with muck all over it. Again, she produces a tissue and cleans the bird. Afterwards, she hears a voice from the bushes.

"Excuse me, madam," it says. "Do you have any more tissues?"

"No!" the woman replies, offended.

"All right," the voice says. "I'll just have to use another duck, then."

Remember this one?

Customer: I'd like a pair of stockings for my wife.
Storekeeper: Sheer?
Customer: No, she's at home.

If you think it'll help...

A husband and wife visit a counsellor after 15 years of marriage.

The counsellor asks them what the problem is and the wife starts ranting, listing every problem they've had during their marriage. She goes on and on and on. Suddenly the counsellor gets up, walks around the desk and kisses her passionately. The woman shuts up immediately and sits in a daze. The counsellor turns to the husband and says, "This is what your wife needs at least three times a week. Can you do this?"

The husband thinks for a moment and replies, "Well, I can drop her off here on Mondays and Wednesdays, but on Fridays I'm out drinking."

What does an Aussie use for protection during sex? A bus shelter.

And that's magic

Three Essex girls are flying back from an exotic holiday when their plane crashes into the sea. The three survive and are washed up on a deserted island. They've been stranded for days when they find a magic lamp. They rub it and eventually a genie pops out.

"Since I can only grant three wishes," he says, "you may each have one."

Number one says, "I've been stuck here for days. I miss my family, my husband, and my life. I just want to go home."

She disappears in a flash and is returned to her family.

Number two then says, "I've been stuck here for days as well. I miss my local boozer and Friday night kebabs. I want to go home too."

She vanishes as well and finds herself back down the pub.

Suddenly, number three starts crying uncontrollably.

The genie asks, "My dear, what's the matter?"

She whimpers, "I'm lonely. I wish my mates were still here."

Cold reception

A woman walks into an ice cream parlour and orders a scoop of chocolate ice cream.

The owner shakes his head apologetically and says, "I'm sorry, but we're all out of chocolate."

The lady looks confused and gazes down through the glass at all the ice cream tubs and then looks back up at the man and asks for a cornet of chocolate ice cream. The man replies a little annoyed, "Er, I'm sorry, but we're all out of chocolate."

The lady then seems to get the point and walks down to the end of the parlour. She then looks back up and says, "Excuse me? Can I get a litre of chocolate ice cream?"

At this point the owner explodes, "Miss, do me a favour please? Can you spell the 'straw' in strawberry?"

"Sure," says the woman. "S-T-R-A-W."

"Now can you spell the 'van' in vanilla?" says the owner.

"Yes. V-A-N," the lady says confidently.

"Now can you spell the f*ck in chocolate?" the owner says smartly.

The lady looks up at the ceiling in thought then replies, "There is no f*ck in chocolate."

"Exactly!" screams the owner.

Lady garden

A man and a woman started to have sex in the middle of a dark forest. After about 15 minutes of it, the man finally gets up and says, "Damn, I wish I had a torch!"

The woman says, "Me too; you've been eating grass for the past ten minutes!"

Role model

Three young boys are trying to figure out whose dad is best.

"My dad is so good he can shoot an arrow, run after it, get in front of it and catch it in his bare hands," says the first lad.

"My dad is so good that he can shoot a gun, run after the bullet, get in front of it and catch it in his bare hands," says the second lad.

"I've got you both beat," says the third lad. "My dad works for the council, and he's so good he can get off work at five and be home by 4:30!"

Salesmanship

The flower vendor is an old hand at unloading his last few bunches each day. Appealing to a businessman on his way home, the vendor says, "How about a nice bunch of roses to surprise your wife?"

"Haven't got a wife," the businessman responds.

"Then how about some carnations for your girlfriend?" the vendor proposes without missing a beat.

"Haven't got a girlfriend."

The vendor breaks into a big smile. "Oh, then you'll want all the flowers I've got left. You have a lot to celebrate!"

The other half

A man starts a new job, and his boss says, "If you marry my daughter, I'll make you a partner and give you a £1million salary."

The man's puzzled, until he sees a picture of the girl – she makes Margaret Thatcher look hot. But after a moment he accepts, figuring the money's worth it, and they get married.

A year later the fella's up on a ladder hanging a picture and yells to his wife, "Bring me my hammer, please."

She mumbles, "Get the hammer, get the hammer," and grudgingly fetches the hammer.

The guy says, "Can you hand me the nails, please?"

She mumbles, "Get me some nails, get me some nails," and does so.

The guy starts hammering, hits his thumb, and yells, "Ow! F**k me!"

She shuffles off, mumbling, "Get the bag, get the bag..."

Land that time forgot

After living in the remote wilderness of Norfolk all his life, an old man decides it's finally time to visit Norwich. In one of the shops he picks up a mirror and looks in it.

Not knowing what it is, he remarks, "How about that? Here's a picture of my dead daddy."

He buys the 'picture', but on the way home he remembers his wife, Lizzy, didn't like his father, so he hangs it in the barn, and every morning before leaving for the fields, he goes there to look at it. Lizzy begins to get suspicious of these many trips to the barn. One day after her husband leaves, she searches the barn and finds the mirror.

As she looks into the glass, she fumes, "So that's the ugly bitch he's runnin' around with..."

Easy, tiger

Some friends are playing a round of golf when they hear shouts in the distance. Looking across, they watch, amazed, as a buxom lady runs on to the fairway, pulls off some of her clothes and sprints up the course. Not two minutes later, two men in white coats appear and ask which way the woman has gone. They point up the course and the two men run off in that direction.

Bemused, the golfers carry on with their game, but are again disturbed by another man. This time he's staggering over the hill, panting with the effort of carrying two buckets of sand. Between wheezes, the newcomer, too, asks which way the woman has gone and then totters away. Increasingly baffled, the golf party runs after the figure. "What the hell is going on?" they ask.

Gasping, the man explains. "That woman has escaped from our treatment clinic. She has acute nymphomania, and as soon as she gets all her clothes off, the nearest man is ravished."

"But why do you need two buckets of sand?" shout the golfers after him.

"Well, I caught her the last time she escaped," pants the man, "so it's my turn for the handicap."

Life's little joke

Two men waiting at the Pearly Gates strike up a conversation.

"How'd you die?" the first man asks the second.

"I froze to death," says the second.

"That's awful," says the first man. "How does it feel to freeze to death?"

"It's very uncomfortable at first," says the second man. "You get the shakes, and you get pains in all your fingers and toes. But, eventually, it's a very calm way to go. You get numb and you kind of drift off, as if you're sleeping. How about you, how did you die?"

"I had a heart attack," says the first man. "You see, I knew my wife was cheating on me, so one day I showed up at home unexpectedly. I ran up to the bedroom and found her alone, knitting. I ran down to the basement, but no one was hiding there, either. I ran up to the second floor, but no one was hiding there either. I ran as fast as I could to the attic, and just as I got there, I had a massive heart attack and died."

The second man shakes his head. "That's so ironic," he says.

"What do you mean?" asks the first man.

"If you'd only stopped to look in the freezer, we'd both still be alive."

Somebody's got to do it

A tourist in Egypt gets chatting to a man in a bar.

"What do you do for a living," asks the traveller.

"I'm a camel castrator," replies the Egyptian.

"Really? How do you go about castrating a camel?" asks the bewildered tourist.

"Well," says the man, "you go behind him and spread his legs. Then you take a big rock in each hand and smack his testicles between the rocks."

"Bugger me! That must hurt," says the tourist.

"Not if you keep your thumbs out of the way."

The joy of sex

After marrying a younger woman, a middle-aged man finds that no matter what he does in the sack, she never achieves orgasm. So he visits his doctor for advice. "Maybe fantasy is the solution," says the doctor. "Why not hire a strapping young man and, while you two are making love, have him wave a towel over you?"

The doctor smiles. "Make sure he's totally naked; that way your wife can fantasise her way to a full-blown orgasm."

Optimistic, he returns home and hires a handsome young escort. But it's no use; even when the stud stands naked, waving the towel, the wife remains unsatisfied. Perplexed, the man returns to his doctor.

"Try reversing it for a while," says the quack. "Have the young man make love to your wife and you wave the towel over them."

And so he returns home to try again, this time waving the towel as the same escort pumps away enthusiastically. Soon, the wife has an enormous, screaming orgasm. Smiling, the husband drops the towel and taps the young man on the shoulder.

"You see?" he shouts triumphantly. "That's how you wave a bloody towel."

How do you spot a rebel Amish teenager?
He has a secret stash of pictures of women without bonnets.

Dog food

One day, a little 5'1" guy walks into a pub and asks: "Excuse me; does anyone here own a big Rottweiler?"

A 7'1" man stands up and says: "That's Tyson. He's mine; why?"

"I think my dog has killed yours," says the pipsqueak, eyeing the big guy nervously.

"I don't believe it," says the hard lad. "What breed is your dog? Doberman? Pit Bull?"

"No, it's a Chihuahua," says the man.

"How can a Chihuahua kill a Rottweiler?" asks the owner.

"It got stuck in your dog's throat," replies the little fella.

Little bastard!

Standing at a urinal, a man notices a midget is watching him. The man doesn't feel uncomfortable until the midget drags a small stepladder over to him, climbs it, and proceeds to admire the man's privates close up. "Wow!" says the little fella. "I bet you don't have any problem with the ladies."

Surprised and flattered, the man thanks the midget and starts to move away. But the little man stops him. "I know this is a strange request, but can I take a closer look?"

Before the man can stop him, the wee man reaches out and tightly grabs the man's testicles. "OK," he shouts. "Hand over your wallet or I'll jump."

Going too far

A shaven-headed Britney Spears goes to a psychiatrist to seek help.

"I don't know what to do," says the bald-headed pop princess. "My life's a complete mess."

The shrink looks over his glasses at her and says, "Your current antics are a cry for help, Miss Spears. After all you've been in the limelight most of your life, starting with the Mickey Mouse Club."

Suddenly, Spears stands up and shouts, "How dare you! I've never played for Arsenal!"

Ask a silly question

At 7am, a lone wife hears a key in the front door. She wanders down, bleary-eyed, to find her husband in the kitchen – drunk, with ruffled hair and lipstick on his collar. "I assume," she snarls, "that there's a very good reason for you to come waltzing in here at seven in the morning?"

"There is," he replies. "Breakfast."

Johnny, remember me

A beautiful woman is driving back to the city when her sports car breaks down. Desperate, she wanders over the fields and spies a farmhouse where she knocks on the door.

"Oh, thank God," she says, when the farmer answers. "My car's broken down. Could I stay the night until someone comes out tomorrow?"

The farmer eyes her suspiciously. "Well, OK," he says "but don't mess with my two sons, Jed and Jake."

Behind him, two strapping young men appear, smiling

sheepishly. The woman agrees, but after going to the guest room, she can't stop thinking about the two young bucks in the next room. Throwing caution to the wind, she quietly tip-toes across.

"Jake! Jed!" she whispers. "Would you like me to teach you the ways of the world?"

"Huh?" comes the reply.

"The only thing is I don't want to get pregnant – so you'll have to wear these condoms."

Beaming, the boys agree and soon embark on a glorious night of saucy three-way passion. Forty years later, Jed and Jake are sitting on their front porch, fondly remembering their erotic experience.

"It was fantastic, but I do have one question" says Jed.

"Oh?" says Jake .

His brother frowns, "Well, do you really care if the woman gets pregnant?"

"Nope," says Jake thoughtfully. "I reckon not."

"Me neither," says Jed. "Let's take these things off."

What do you call a fat alien?
An extra-cholesterol.

Simple, Inuit?

1st Eskimo: Where did your mother come from?
2nd Eskimo: Alaska.
1st Eskimo: Don't bother; I'll ask her myself.

Mind your language

Little 10-year-old Freddie goes for a long weekend with his uncle, a wealthy Hampshire farm-owner. One evening, as Uncle John and his wife are entertaining guests with cocktails, they are interrupted by an out-of-breath Freddie who shouts out, "Uncle John! Come quick! The bull is f**king the cow!"

Uncle John, highly embarrassed, takes young Freddie aside, and explains that a certain amount of decorum is required. "You should have said, 'The bull is surprising the cow' – not some filth picked up in the playground," he says.

A few days later, Freddie comes in again as his aunt and uncle are entertaining guests. "Uncle John! The bull is surprising the cows!"

The adults share a knowing grin.

Uncle John says, "Thank you Freddie, but surely you meant to say the cow, not cows. A bull cannot surprise more than one cow at a time, you know…"

"Yes, he can!" replies his nephew. "He's f**king the horse!"

Getting his backup

Jesus and Satan are having an ongoing argument about who's better on their computers. Finally, God says, "I am going to set up a test which will take two hours and I will judge who does the better job."

So Satan and Jesus sit down at the keyboards and type away. They do everything their PCs can handle. But, ten minutes before the time's up, lightning suddenly flashes across the sky and the electricity goes off.

Satan stares at his blank screen and screams every curse word known in the underworld. Jesus just sighs. The electricity finally flickers back on and each of them reboots.

Satan starts searching, frantically screaming, "It's gone! It's all gone! I lost everything when the power went out!"

Meanwhile, Jesus quietly starts printing out all his files from the past two hours. Satan sees this and becomes even more irate. "Wait! He cheated! How did he do it!?"

God shrugs and says, "Jesus saves."

Freezer jolly good fellow

Seventy-year-old George goes for his annual check-up. He tells the doctor that he feels fine, but often has to go to the bathroom during the night. Then he says: "But you know, Doc: I'm blessed. God knows my eyesight is going, so he puts on the light when I pee and turns it off when I'm done!"

A little later in the day, Dr. Smith calls George's wife and says: "Your husband's test results were fine, but he said something strange that has been bugging me. He claims that God turns the light on and off for him when he uses the bathroom at night."

Thelma exclaims: "That old fool! He's been peeing in the refrigerator again!"

Last rites

A priest is preparing a man for his passing over. Whispering firmly, the priest says, "Denounce the devil! Let him know how little you think of him!"

The dying man says nothing. The priest repeats his order. Still the man says nothing.

The priest asks, "Why do you refuse to denounce the devil and his evil?"

The dying man replies, "Until I know for sure where I'm headed, I don't think I ought to aggravate anybody."

Salt and vinegar?

A man goes into a fish and chip shop and says, "Can I have fish and chips twice, please?"

The shop owner says, "I heard you the first time."

What's the difference between bird flu and Man City?
Bird flu has got to Europe.

Delicate matter

A newlywed couple arrive back from their honeymoon to move into their tiny new flat.

"Care to go to bed?" the husband asks.

"Shh!" says his blushing bride. "These walls are paper-thin; the neighbours will know what you mean! Next time, ask me in code, like: 'Have you left the washing machine door open?' instead."

So, the following night, the husband asks: "I don't suppose you left the washing machine door open, darling?"

"No," she snaps back, "I definitely shut it." Then she rolls over and falls asleep.

The next morning, she wakes up feeling a little frisky herself, so she nudges her husband and says: "I think I did leave the washing machine door open after all..."

"Don't worry," says the man. "It was only a small load, so I did it by hand."

Gallant allies

During WWII an American soldier has been on the front line in Europe for three months, when he is finally given a week of R & R. He catches a supply boat to a base in the south of England, and then catches a train to London. The train is extremely crowded and he can't find a seat. He is dead on his feet and walks the length of the train looking for any place to sit down. Finally he finds a compartment with seats facing each other; there is room for two people on each seat. On one side sits a proper-looking, older British lady with a small dog sitting in the empty seat beside her.

"Could I please sit in that seat?" asks the Yank.

The lady is insulted. "You bloody Americans are so rude," she says. "Can't you see my dog is sitting there?"

"Lady, I love dogs," says the American. "I have a couple at home – so I would be glad to hold your dog if I could sit down."

The lady replies, "You Americans are not only rude; you are arrogant too."

He leans against the wall for a time, but is so tired he finally says, "Lady, I've been on the front line in Europe for three months with not a decent rest for all that time. Could I please sit there and hold your dog?"

The lady replies, "You Americans are not only rude and arrogant; you are also obnoxious!"

With that comment, the soldier calmly steps in, picks up the dog, throws it out of the window and sits down. The lady is speechless.

An older, neatly dressed Englishman sitting across on the other seat suddenly says, "Young man, I do not know if all you Americans fit the lady's description of you or not, but I do know that you Americans do a lot of things wrong. You drive on the wrong side of the road, you hold your fork with the wrong hand and now you have just thrown the wrong bitch out of the window."

Vegging out

A guy walks into a watchmaker's shop and asks the man behind the counter for a potato clock.

"A potato clock?" says the watchmaker. "I've never heard of a potato clock. Why do you want one?"

The customer sighs. "Well, you see," he says, "I went for a job interview yesterday and was offered the job. So I asked the boss what time I should start and he said nine o'clock."

"So?" asks the kindly old shopkeeper.

"Well," replies the man, "he said to do that, I'll need to get a potato clock."

Playing the game

A man walks up to a woman and asks, "Would you sleep with me for £1,000,000?"

She quickly replies, "Yes."

So then he asks, "Would you sleep with me for £20?"

Astounded by the question, she says, "Of course not. What kind of woman do you think I am?"

He says, "Well, we've already determined that. Now I'm just working on a price."

Not right in the head

A woman goes to see her GP about something that has been troubling her for some time.

"Doctor, I keep thinking I'm a cartoon character," she says. "One day it's Mickey Mouse, the next it's Donald Duck. This morning I woke up and I was convinced I was Bambi."

"Well," replies the Doc. "It just sounds to me like you're having Disney spells."

About to snap

A photographer for a national magazine is assigned to get photos of a great forest fire. Smoke at the scene is too thick to get any good shots, so he frantically calls his office to hire a plane.

"It will be waiting for you at the airport!" he is assured by his editor. As soon as he gets to the small, rural airport, sure enough, a plane is warming up near the runway. He jumps in with his equipment and yells, "Let's go! Let's go!" The pilot swings the plane into the wind and soon they are airborne.

"Fly over the north side of the fire," says the photographer, "and make three or four low-level passes."

"Why?" asks the pilot.

"Because I'm going to take pictures! I'm a photographer and photographers take pictures!" says the photographer with great exasperation.

After a long gulp, the pilot says, "You mean you're not the instructor?"

Absent friends

A man moves to New York City from Suffolk, leaving two of his best friends behind. To keep their tradition of nightly drinks alive, every night he goes to a British-themed pub and orders three pints. After a month of this the barman is curious and asks the man what he's doing. Touched by his story, the barman has the three pints ready for the man every time he comes in. One day, the man tells the barman to only give him two pints.

"My condolences," says the bartender, thinking that one of the man's friends has died.

"No, no," says the man, "they're both still alive. I've just quit drinking."

White man speak with forked tongue

The Lone Ranger is riding through the mountains when Indians attack. They drag him from his horse and bury him in the sand up to his neck, ready to kill him. Knowing he's about to kick the bucket, the Lone Ranger calls his horse over and whispers in his ear. The horse gallops off and returns a few minutes later with a gorgeous naked blonde girl on its back.

After surveying the scene she hops down out of the saddle and sits on his face, sighing and moaning as she writhes about. When she's finished the Indians dive in for the kill.

"Stop! I just want one more word with my horse," cries the Lone Ranger.

They agree and his steed trots over to hear his final words.

"I said 'posse', you useless tw*t!"

Old retainer

A man was passing a country estate and saw a sign on the gate. It read: "Please ring bell for the caretaker." He rang the bell and an old man appeared.

"Are you the caretaker?" the fellow asked.

"Yes, I am," replied the old man. "What do you want?"

"I'd just like to know why you can't ring the bell yourself."

It's an ill wind...

James Blunt, Westlife, Justin Timberlake and the Pussycat Dolls are on a sinking ship. Who gets saved?

The world of music.

Necessary evil

An Amish woman is driving her horse and buggy down the road when she gets pulled over.

"You have a broken reflector on your buggy," the policeman says, "but more importantly, one of your reins is looped around your horse's balls. That's cruelty to animals. Have your husband take care of that right away!"

Later that day, the woman tells her husband, "A policeman pulled me over today for two reasons. First, he said the reflector was broken."

"Well, that's easily fixed," says her husband. "What else?"

"I'm not sure: something about the emergency brake."

And justice for all

On trial in a rural American town, an English man thinks he has no chance of getting off a murder charge, despite his innocence. So, shortly before the jury retires, he bribes one of the jurors to find him guilty of the lesser crime of manslaughter.

The jury is out for over three days before eventually returning a verdict of manslaughter.

The relieved defendant collars the bribed juror and says: "Thanks. However did you manage it?"

"It wasn't easy," admits the juror. "All the others wanted to acquit you."

Doctor's dilemma

An 85-year-old man goes to his doctor's to get a sperm count.

The doctor gives him a jar and says: "Take this jar home and bring back a semen sample tomorrow."

The next day the old boy reappears at the doctor's office and gives him the jar, which is as clean and empty as on the previous day. The doctor asks what happened and the man explains: "Well, doc, it's like this: first I tried with my right hand, but nothing. Then I tried with my left hand, but still nothing. Then I asked my wife for help. She tried with her right hand, her left, with her mouth, first with the teeth in, then with her teeth out and still nothing. We even called up Arlene, our neighbour, and she tried too, with both hands, then an armpit and she even tried squeezing it between her knees, but still nothing."

The doctor is shocked. "You asked your neighbor?"

The old man replies, "Yep. And no matter what we tried, we still couldn't get the jar open."

Rotten to macaw

A woman's dishwasher breaks down, so she calls a repairman. Since she has to go to work the next day, she tells the repairman, "I'll leave the key under the mat. Fix the dishwasher, leave the bill on the counter and I'll send you a cheque in the post. Oh, by the way; don't worry about my bulldog. He won't bother you. But, whatever you do, do not, under any circumstances talk to my parrot! I repeat, do not talk to my parrot!"

When the repairman arrives at the woman's apartment the following day, he discovers the biggest, meanest-looking bulldog he has ever seen. But, just as the woman warns, the dog

just lies there on the carpet watching the repairman go about his work. The parrot, however, is driving the man nuts the whole time with his incessant yelling, cursing and name-calling.

Finally the repairman can contain himself no longer and yells, "Shut up, you stupid, ugly bird!"

The parrot replies, "Get him, Spike."

What's six inches long, with a head on it, that women like to blow?
Money.

Fishy business

A man calls home to his wife and says, "Honey, I've been asked to go fishing with my boss and several of his friends. We'll be gone for a week. This is a good opportunity for me to get that promotion I've been wanting. We're leaving from the office and I'll swing by the house to pick my things up. Oh – please pack my new blue silk pyjamas."

The wife thinks this sounds a little suspicious, but being a good wife she does exactly what her husband asked. The following weekend he comes home a little tired, but otherwise looking good.

The wife welcomes him home and asks if he caught many fish.

He says, "Loads! But why didn't you pack my new blue silk pyjamas like I asked you to do?"

The wife replies, "I did. They were in your tackle box…"

Give and take

Four blokes are making the most of a fine Sunday with a round of golf. During the fourth hole they discuss how they actually got away from their wives for the day.

First bloke: "You have no idea what I had to do to be able to come out golfing this weekend. I had to promise my wife that I'd paint every room in the house next weekend."

Second bloke: "That's nothing, I had to promise my wife that I'd build her a new deck for the pool."

Third bloke: "Man, you both have it easy! I had to promise my wife that I'd remodel the kitchen for her."

They continue to play the hole when they realise that the fourth bloke hasn't said a word. So they ask him. "You haven't said anything about what you had to do to be able to come golfing this weekend. What's the deal?"

The fourth bloke replies: "I just set my alarm for 5:30 am. When it goes off I give the wife a nudge and say, 'Golf course or intercourse?' So she says: 'Remember to wear your sweater, dear.'"

How did the redneck die drinking milk?
The cow sat on him.

Countrymen

Tony Blair calls John Prescott into his office and says, "John, I have a great idea! We are going to go all-out to win back rural Britain."

"Great idea, Tony," says Prezza. "How will we go about it?"

"Well," says Blair, "we'll get ourselves tweed jackets, some wellies, a stick, a flat cap and a Labrador. Then we'll really look the part. We'll go to a nice old country pub, in one of those posh villages, and we'll prove we really enjoy the countryside."

"Right," says Prescott.

So a few days later, all kitted out and with the requisite Labrador at heel, they set off from London in a westerly direction. Eventually they find a lovely country pub and go up to the bar.

"Good evening landlord, may we have two pints of your best ale?" says Blair.

"Good evening, Prime Minister," says the landlord, "two pints of best it is, coming up."

Blair and Prescott stand by the bar drinking their beer and chatting, nodding now and again to those who come in for a drink.

The dog lies quietly at their feet when, all of a sudden, the door from the adjacent bar opens and in walks an old shepherd, complete with crook. He goes up to the Labrador, lifts its tail and looks underneath, shrugs his shoulders and walks back to the other bar. Moments later, another old shepherd comes in with his crook and repeats what the first shepherd did before scratching his head and going back to the other bar. Over the course of the next half hour or so several other locals come in, lift the dog's tail and go away looking puzzled. Eventually Blair and Prescott can stand it no longer and call the landlord over.

"Tell me," says Blair, "why do all these old shepherds and locals come in and look under the dog's tail like that? Is it a local custom?"

"Good Lord, no," says the landlord. "It's just that word spread to the other bar that there was a Labrador in this bar with two arseholes."

Like father, like son

A little boy was lost in the supermarket. He went up to the security guard and said: "I've lost my dad."

The security guard asked him, "What's he like?"

The little boy replied, "Beer, kebabs and big tits."

Putting the boot in

Bill Gates is hanging out with the chairman of Ferrari.

"If automotive technology had kept pace with computer technology over the past few decades," boasts Gates, "you would now be driving a V-32 instead of a V-8. It would have a top speed of 10,000 miles per hour and only cost £50."

"Sure," says the Ferrari chairman. "But would you really want to drive a car that crashes four times a day?"

Moving traffic violation

A man was pulled over by the police one day because his car didn't have any hubcaps on his tyres.

"What's the charge, officer?" asked the man.

The cop replied, "Indecent exposure."

"Indecent exposure!" exclaimed the fella.

The cop responded, "Yes! You can't just ride around with your nuts showing!"

Well, whaddaya know?

A man was on holiday in Kenya. While he was walking through the bush, he came across an elephant standing with one leg raised in the air. The elephant seemed distressed, so the man approached it, very carefully. He got down on one knee and inspected the elephant's foot. There was a large thorn deeply embedded in the bottom of the foot. As carefully and as gently as he could he removed the thorn, and the elephant gingerly put down its foot. The elephant turned to face the man and, with a rather stern look on its face, stared at him.

For a good ten minutes the man stood frozen, thinking of nothing else but being trampled. Eventually the wrinkly-skinned mammal trumpeted loudly, turned and walked away.

Years later, the man was walking through the zoo with his son. As they approached the elephant enclosure, one of the creatures turned and walked over to where they were standing at the rail. It stared at him and the man couldn't help wondering if this was the same elephant. After a while it trumpeted loudly, then it continued to stare at him. The man summoned up his courage, climbed over the railing and made his way into the enclosure. He walked right up to the elephant and stared back in wonder. Suddenly the elephant trumpeted again, wrapped its trunk around one of the man's legs and swung him wildly back and forth along the railing, killing him.

Probably wasn't the same elephant.

How do historians know the Indians were the first people in America?
They've seen their reservations.

Try, try again

In Jerusalem, a female CNN journalist hears about a very old Jewish man who has been going to the Wailing Wall to pray, twice a day, every day for years. So she goes to check it out. She walks to the Wailing Wall and there he is walking slowly up to the holy site. She watches him pray and after about 45 minutes, when he turns to leave, she approaches him for an interview.

"I'm Rebecca Smith from CNN. Sir, how long have you been coming to the Wailing Wall and praying?" she begins.

"For about 60 years," says the old fella.

"60 years! That's amazing! What do you pray for?"

"I pray for peace between the Muslims and the Jews. I pray for all the hatred to stop and I pray for all our children to grow up in safety and friendship," says the wizened old gent.

"How do you feel after doing this for 60 years?"

"Like I'm talking to a brick wall."

One liner

A wee Scottish man has worked in the Clyde shipyards all his life. He wins the lottery and decides to take his wife on a trip on one of the ships he helped build – the QE2. As it's a once-in-a-lifetime event, he goes the whole hog and takes one of the best rooms. Naturally, the captain hears one of the men who built the QE2 is on board and the couple are invited to the captain's table at dinner.

The couple is sat next to an immensely wealthy lady at dinner who asks: "Have you sailed on the ship many times before?"

"Naw," says the Scottish fella's wife, "This is oor furst time!"

"Oh, I see," drawls the lady. "My husband and I make this trip three times every year."

"Three times? Every year?" squeaks the wee worker's wife, "How d'ye manage it?"

The lady coughs politely and says, "My husband works for Cunard, you know."

"Weell!" spits out the Scottish woman, "Mah man works f*ckin hard tae, but we don't brag aboot it!"

Bungle in the jungle

One fine day in the forest, Mr Rabbit is on his daily run when he sees a giraffe rolling a joint.

"Oh, Mr Giraffe!" he calls. "Why do you do drugs? Come run with me instead!" So the giraffe stops rolling and runs with the rabbit.

Then they come across an elephant doing lines of cocaine.

"Oh, Mr Elephant, why do you do drugs? Come run with us instead." So the elephant stops snorting and goes running with the other two animals.

Then they spy a lion preparing a syringe. "Oh, Mr Lion," cries the rabbit, "why do you do drugs? Come run with us instead."

But no – with a mighty roar, the lion smashes the rabbit to smithereens. "No!" cry the giraffe and elephant. "Why did you do that? All he was trying to do was help you out!"

The lion growls. "That rabbit always makes me run around the forest when he's whizzing his tits off."

Well, he asked for it

Alan Pardew goes into the local supermarket and sees an old lady struggling with heavy shopping bags.

"Can you manage?" asks the boss of Charlton FC.

"No chance!" she replies angrily. "You got yourself into this mess; you can get yourself out of it!"

A keen eye

A man applies for a job in a Florida lemon grove but seems to have no experience whatsoever.

The foreman is puzzled and says to the man, "I'm not sure that I can employ you because you just don't have the experience. Have you ever picked lots of lemons before?"

At this the man gets up and shouts, "What are you talking about? Don't you recognise me? I'm Alan Curbishley! I manage West Ham!"

Advance planning

After 50 years of marriage to Lena, Ole becomes very ill and realises that he will soon die. In bed one night, Ole turns to his wife.

"Lena," he asks. "When I am gone, do you think you will marry another man?"

Lena gives it some thought. "Well, yes," she says. "Marriage has been good to me and I think that I will surely marry again."

Ole is taken aback. "Why, Lena," he cries, "will you bring your new husband into our house?"

"This is a fine house," says Lena. "Yes, I think we will live here."

"But Lena," Ole gasps, "will you bring your new husband into our bed?"

Lena replies, "Well, yes; you made this bed, a good strong bed. Yes! Sure I will bring my new husband into this bed."

Ole gulps. "But Lena," he says in a quiet voice. "You won't let your new husband use my golf clubs, will you?"

Lena smiles at her husband. "Oh, Ole!" she grins, misty-eyed. "Of course he won't use your golf clubs! He's left-handed."

A small kindness

One afternoon, a wealthy lawyer is riding in the back of his limousine when he sees two men eating grass by the roadside. He orders his driver to stop and he gets out to investigate.

"Why are you eating grass?" he asks one man.

"We don't have any money for food," the poor man replies.

"Oh, come along with me then."

"But sir, I have a wife with two children!"

"Bring them along! And you, come with us too!" he says to the other man.

"But sir, I have a wife with six children!" the second man answers.

"Bring them as well!"

They all climb into the car, which is no easy task, even with a car as large as the limo. Once under way, one of the poor fellows says, "Sir, you are too kind. Thank you for taking all of us with you."

The lawyer replies, "No problem; the grass at my home is about two feet tall!"

Holy see

One day the Pope decides he's had enough of the 'No sex' rule, so he decides to treat himself to a bit of five-on-one in his bedroom. Half-way through, a window cleaner appears at his window and demands £5,000 to keep schtum, so the Pope pays him. A week later a cardinal comes round and notices how clean the windows are.

"How much did your window cleaner charge?" he asks.

"£5,000," the Pope replies.

"Christ, he must have seen you coming!"

Crap presents

Young Justin has a swearing problem and his father's getting tired of it.

He decides to ask a shrink what to do. The shrink says, "Negative reinforcement. Since Christmas is coming up, ask Justin what he wants from Santa. If he swears while he tells you his wish list, leave a pile of dog poop in place of each gift he requests."

Two days before Christmas, Justin's father asks him what he wants for Christmas. "I want a damn teddy bear lying beside me when I wake up. When I go downstairs, I want to see a damn train going around the damn tree. And when I go outside, I want to see a damn bike leaning up against the damn garage."

On Christmas morning, Justin wakes up and rolls into a pile of dog poop. Confused, he walks downstairs and sees another pile under the tree. He walks outside, looks at a huge pile of dog poo by the garage and walks inside. His dad smiles and asks, "What did Santa bring you this year?"

Justin replies, "I think I got a goddamn dog, but I can't find the son of a bitch!"

Just got worse

There's this little man sitting in a pub, just staring into his beer. He stays like that for half an hour. Then this skinhead comes into the pub, goes straight up to the guy, steals his drink and downs it in one. The little man starts crying.

Taken aback and feeling a bit guilty, the skinhead comes over all concerned. "Come on, fella," he says. "It's not that bad, is it?"

The man looks up at him and says, "Today is the worst day

of my life. First, I overslept and was late for an important meeting at work. My boss fired me. When I was escorted from the building on the way to my car, I realised it had been stolen. I got a cab home and because I was early I caught my wife in bed with my best friend. I left home and came down the pub. And then, just as I was about to end it all, you show up and drink my f*cking arsenic!"

> How do you know if there's a fighter pilot at a party?
> He'll tell you.

Happy release

Brenda is at home making dinner, when her husband's work mate Bill arrives at her door.

"Brenda, can I come in?" he asks. "I've something to tell you."

"Of course you can come in. But where's my husband?" enquires Brenda.

"That's what I'm here to tell you, Brenda. There was an accident down at the Guinness brewery."

"Oh, God, no!" cries Brenda. "Please don't tell me."

"I must, Brenda. Your husband is dead and gone. I'm sorry."

Finally, she looks up at Bill. "How did it happen?"

"It was terrible, Brenda. He fell into a vat of Guinness and drowned."

"Oh, my dear Jesus! Did he at least go quickly?" sobbed Brenda.

"Well, no, Brenda. Fact is, he got out three times to pee."

The lady is a tramp

A lady is walking down the street when a particularly shabby-looking homeless woman asks her for a couple of quid. The woman takes out a fiver and asks, "If I give you this money, will you buy some wine with it instead of dinner?"

"No, I had to stop drinking years ago," the homeless woman replies.

"Will you use it to go shopping instead of buying food?" the woman questions again.

"No, I don't waste time shopping," the homeless woman replies. "I need to spend all my time trying to stay alive."

"Will you spend this on a beauty salon instead of food?" the woman asks.

"Are you nuts?" replies the homeless woman. "I haven't had my hair done in 20 years!"

"Well," says the woman, "I'm not going to give you the money. Instead, I'm going to take you out for dinner with my husband and myself tonight."

The homeless woman is astounded. "Won't your husband be furious with you for doing that? I know I'm dirty and I probably smell pretty disgusting."

The woman replies, "That's OK. It's important for him to see what a woman looks like after she's given up shopping, hair appointments and wine."

What are woks for?
Throwing at wabbits.

Why was the exhibitionist drinking window-
cleaning fluid?
To stop himself from streaking.

Unkindest cut of all

A little old lady walks down the street, dragging two plastic
rubbish bags with her, one in each hand. There's a hole in one
of the bags and every once in a while a £20 note flies out of it
on to the pavement.

Noticing this, a policeman stops her.

"Ma'am, there are £20 notes falling out of that bag."

"Damn!" says the little old lady. "I'd better go back and see if
I can still find some. Thanks for the warning!"

"Well, now, not so fast," says the cop. "How did you get all
that money? Did you steal it?"

"Oh, no," says the little old lady. "You see, my back yard
backs up to the car park of the football stadium and each time
there's a game, a lot of fans come and pee in the bushes, right
into my flowerbeds! So I go and stand behind the bushes with
a big hedge clipper and each time someone sticks his little
thingie through the bushes, I say: '£20 or off it comes!'"

"Hey, not a bad idea!" laughs the cop. "By the way, what's in
the other bag?"

"Well," says the little old lady, "not all of them pay."

Bum's gone to Iceland

What do Eskimos get from sitting on the ice too long?
Polaroids.

Man's best friend

In the middle of the night, a man phones the local vet to tell him his dog has swallowed a condom.

"You've got to help me," cries the man. "I don't know what to do."

"It's rather late," says the vet, "but, as it's an emergency, I'll be there as soon as I can."

"Hurry, please," says the owner.

"What should I do in the meantime?"

"Just keep the dog as still as you can," says the vet. "I'll get there as soon as possible."

After an hour, the vet is still driving when his mobile rings.

"I phoned earlier," says the caller. "My dog swallowed a condom."

"Yes, I know," replies the vet. "I'm going as fast as I can, but I'm stuck in traffic."

"You needn't bother," says the dog owner.

"Oh, no! Has the animal died?" cries the vet.

"No; we've found another condom in the drawer."

What's the worst thing about Upton Park?
The seats face the pitch.

Frying tonight

A man goes into a fish 'n' chip shop with a salmon under his arm.

He asks "Do you sell fish cakes here?"

"No," comes the reply.

"Shame; it's his birthday."

Trunk and disorderly

A baby boy is born with no arms, no legs and no body but his father still loves him. Eighteen years pass and the father takes his son to the pub for his first pint. The son takes his first sip and immediately he grows a torso, so the father tells him to drink again. The son takes another sip and grows some arms and legs. He's so happy he goes running into the street shouting and waving his arms around when he's suddenly hit by a lorry.

The barman shakes his head sadly. "He should have quit while he was ahead."

In days of old

A brave knight has to go off to fight in the Crusades and leaves his sexy wife at home. As she can't be left alone, he fits her with a very lethal chastity belt made out of razor blades. On his victorious return, he lines up all his male staff and makes them drop their trousers. He is greeted by a whole line of shredded todgers, apart from one. He goes up to the man and says,

"I trusted you, and, unlike all the others, you have not betrayed my trust. In return, I shall give you half my land."

To which the faithful servant replies, "Ugg ou gery muk."

> What's the difference between roast beef and pea soup?
> Anyone can roast beef.

Proof of life

Osama bin Laden appeared on Al Jazeera this morning to quell rumours of his death. To prove that his appearance was not pre-recorded, Osama stated that he "watched the football and England were rubbish".

Government officials have dismissed the report, saying it could have happened any time over the last ten years.

Dumbo and dumber

A man goes to his doctor and asks if there's a way to make his undersized penis any bigger. The doctor says there is a revolutionary surgery where a baby elephant trunk is grafted on to the end of his member. At just £3,000 for the operation the man agrees and six weeks later he's ready to try out his newly enlarged member.

While he is having dinner with his new date he feels an unusual stirring in his trousers and thinks tonight could be the night. They continue chatting over dinner when suddenly his penis flies out of his zipper, steals a bun from the table and disappears insides his trousers once more.

"Wow! Can you do that again?" asks his date, clearly impressed.

"My dick can," the man replies, "but I don't think my arse can take another bread roll."

Delicate instrument

While out on an expedition, a man is climbing over a fallen tree when his shotgun goes off, hitting him straight in the groin. Rushed to hospital, he awakes from his anaesthetic to find the surgeon has done a marvellous job of repairing his damaged member. As he dresses to go home, the surgeon wanders over and hands him a business card.

"This is my brother's card. I'll make an appointment for you to see him."

The guy is shocked. "But it says here that he's a professional flute player. How can he help me?'

The doctor smiles. "Well," he says, "he's going to show you where to put your fingers so that you don't p*ss in your eye."

Birds and the bees

Little Johnny keeps asking his dad for a television in his bedroom, to which his dad keeps saying "No", but after prolonged nagging, the dad agrees.

Several nights later Johnny comes downstairs and asks, "Dad, what's Love Juice?" Dad is horrified and, after looking at Mum, who's also gobsmacked, proceeds to give his son the dreaded sex talk.

Johnny now sits on the sofa with his mouth open in amazement.

Dad asks, "So, what is it you've been watching then, son?"

Johnny replies, "Wimbledon."

What's the Aussie for foreplay?
Brace yourself, Sheila!

Mucky business

Three dustmen are doing their last round before Christmas. The first goes to a house, knocks and finds himself being invited in by a stunning blonde, who takes him upstairs and gives him a good seeing-to.

Afterwards, he rushes out and brags to his two pals about it, so the second decides to try his luck. Sure enough, the same thing happens to him.

Finally, the dustcart driver, reckoning he's on to a sure thing, gets out and knocks on the door. The woman answers, smiles and gives him a fiver.

Severely disappointed, the man asks: 'How come I just get money, when you gave my pals a proper Christmas bonus?'

"Well," the woman replies, "when I asked my husband about tipping you all, he said, 'Give the driver £5 and screw the other two.'"

What's a bloke's idea of doing housework?
Lifting his leg so you can hoover.

Love for sale

Tom, an 80-year-old farmer, is at the doctor's telling him how he's going to marry a mail-order bride.

"How old is the new bride to be?" asks the Doc.

"She'll be 21 in November," Tom proudly proclaims.

Being the wise man that he is, the doctor realises that the sexual appetite of a young woman won't be satisfied by an 80-year-old man and, wanting his old patient's remaining years

to be happy, the doctor tactfully suggests that Tom should consider getting a hired hand to help him out on the farm, knowing nature will take its own course.

About four months later, the doctor runs into Tom on the street.

"How's the new wife?" asks the doctor.

Tom proudly says, "She's pregnant."

The doctor, happy that his sage advice has worked out, continues, "And how's the hired hand?"

Without hesitating, Tom replies, "She's pregnant too!"

Any port in a storm

An Aussie lass goes to her gynaecologist and tells the doctor that no matter how hard she and her husband have tried, she just can't get pregnant.

The doctor says, "OK; take off your clothes and lie down on the table."

The girl sighs and says, "Fair dos, mate: but I was really hoping to have my husband's baby."

His and hearse

A man was passing through a small town when he came upon a huge funeral procession.

"Who died?" he asked a nearby local.

"I'm not sure," replied the local, "but I think it's the one in the coffin."

Keeping it in the family

What do you call the sweat that's produced when a Norfolk couple have sex?

Relative humidity.

Hi, Ena

Wife to husband: "Who was that lady I seen you with last night?"
Husband: "You mean 'I saw.'"
Wife: "OK; who was that eyesore I seen you with last night?"

Can you keep it down?

An Aussie walks into a library and asks the librarian, "Excuse me, mate, can I have a burger and large fries, please?"

Tutting, the bookworm replies, "Excuse me, sir; this is a library."

The Aussie leans over the counter. "I'm sorry, mate," he whispers. "Can I have a burger and large fries, please?"

Notional Elf Service

A man walks into the doctor and says, "I have a recurring dream in which I'm writing *Lord of the Rings*. It's really disturbing."

The doctor says, "I'm afraid you're Tolkien in your sleep."

Clinical finishing

Saddam Hussein is found guilty at his trial and is asked by the judge if he has any final wishes.

"I want to choose my firing squad," demands the dictator.

"I guess that would be OK," replies the judge.

"Great," says Saddam. "I want Lampard, Gerrard and Carragher from 12 yards."

Oldest trick in the book

A minister is winding up his sermon one Sunday in church.

"Next Sunday I am going to preach on the subject of liars:

and in this connection, as a preparation for my discourse, I would like you all to read the 17th chapter of Mark," he says.

On the following Sunday, the vicar walks to the front of the church and says, "Now, then, all of you who have done as I requested and read the 17th chapter of Mark, please raise your hands."

Nearly every hand in the congregation shoots up.

The vicar looks stern and says, "You are the ones I want to talk to about lying. There is no 17th chapter of Mark."

Wonderful for her age

Three sisters aged 92, 94 and 96 live in a house together. One night the 96-year-old runs a bath. She puts her foot in and pauses. She yells to the other sisters, "Was I getting in or out of the bath?"

The 94-year-old yells back, "I don't know. I'll come up and see."

She starts up the stairs and pauses, "Was I going up the stairs or down?" she shouts.

The 92-year-old is sitting at the kitchen table having tea listening to her sisters. She shakes her head and says, "I sure hope I never get that forgetful... knock on wood."

She then yells, "I'll come up and help both of you as soon as I see who's at the door."

What's the similarity between students and sperm?
Only one in a million turns out useful.

Survival of the fittest

Two campers are walking through the woods when a huge brown bear suddenly appears in the clearing about 50 feet in front of them. The bear sees the campers and begins to head towards them. The first guys drops his backpack, digs out a pair of trainers and frantically begins to put them on.

The second guy says: "What are you doing? Trainers won't help you outrun that bear."

"I don't need to outrun the bear," the first bloke says. "I just need to outrun you."

Why does a chicken coop have two doors?
If it had four, it would be a chicken sedan.

Grounds for divorce?

An old woman visits her doctor to ask his help in reviving her husband's libido.

"What about trying Viagra?" asks the doctor.

"Not a chance," she says. "He won't even take an aspirin."

"Not a problem," replies the doctor. "Drop it into his coffee. He won't even taste it. Give it a try and call me in a week to let me know how things went."

Less than a week later she ends up calling the doctor.

"It was horrid: just terrible, doctor," cries the old dear.

"Really? What happened?" asks the doctor.

"Well, I did as you advised and slipped it in his coffee and the effect was almost immediate! He jumped straight up, with

a twinkle in his eye, ripped my clothes to tatters and took me then and there."

"Why so terrible?" asks the doctor, "Was the sex that bad?"

"Oh, no, doctor," says the old lady. "It was the best sex I've had in 25 years! But I'll never be able to show my face in Starbucks again."

Prune in autumn

Two old men are sitting outside the town hall, where a flower show is in progress. One complains, "Cripes, life is boring. We never have any fun! For £10, I'll streak naked through the flower show!"

"You're on!" the other geriatric shouts.

The first old man fumbles out of his clothes and streaks through the hall. Waiting outside, his friend hears a commotion, followed by applause. Then the naked old man bursts through the door, surrounded by a cheering crowd. "How did it go?" asks the friend.

"Great!" says the wrinkled streaker. "I won first prize for dried arrangement!"

Good book

A priest who has to spend the night in a hotel asks the girl in reception to come up to his room for dinner.

After a while he makes a pass at her, but she stops him and reminds him that he is a holy man.

"It's OK," he replies, "it's written in the Bible."

After a wild night of sex she asks to see where in the Bible it says it's OK.

The priest rolls over, takes the Gideon bible out of the desk by the bed and shows her the first page. On it, someone has scrawled: "The girl in reception will shag anyone."

Fitting right in

A bright young Scottish lad named Gordie has the opportunity to go to university in London, so he packs his bags, says goodbye to his mother and leaves the highlands for the big city. After the first week his mother calls to see how her boy is holding up.

"I love it here Mother," Gordie tells her, "but these English students are the oddest people ever! Why, the boy who lives in the dormitory room next to me bangs his head against the wall until midnight every night. And the boy in the room above me stomps around until midnight every night. And the boy right below me blasts his stereo until midnight every night."

"Why don't you complain to the Dean of Students?" asks his mother.

"Well, it doesn't bother me much," answers Gordie. "I'm usually up until that time practising my bagpipes anyway."

Filled with the holy spirit

Jade Goody is looking in a mirror and her fluctuating weight is depressing her. In an act of desperation, she decides to call on God for help. "God if you take away my love handles, I'll devote my life to you," she prays. And just like that, her ears fall off.

Extreme lengths

An extremely drunk man looking for a brothel stumbles blindly into a chiropodist's office instead. He weaves over to the receptionist. Without looking up, she waves him over to the examination bed.

"Stick it through that curtain," she says. Looking forward to something kinky, the drunk whips out his penis and sticks it through the crack in the curtains.

"That's not a foot!" screams the receptionist.

"Christ!" replies the drunk. "I didn't know you had a minimum."

If only they could talk

Little Johnny is sitting in a biology class and the teacher says that an interesting phenomenon of nature is that only humans stutter; no other animal in the world does this. Johnny's hand shoots up.

"Not correct, Miss!" he says.

"Please explain, Johnny," replies the teacher.

"Well, Miss, the other day I was playing with my cat. The neighbours' pitbull came around the corner, and my cat went 'fffffffff! fffffffffff! ffffffffff!', and before he could say 'f*ck off!', the dog ate him!"

What do men and money in the bank have in common?
Both lose interest after withdrawal.

It's Miller time

After striking gold in Alaska, a lonely miner walks down from the mountains and into a saloon in the nearest town.

"I'm lookin' for the meanest, toughest, roughest hooker you got," he says to the barman.

"We got her," he replies. "She's upstairs in the second room on the right."

The miner hands the pint-puller a gold nugget to pay for the lady of the night and two beers. He grabs the bottles, stomps up the stairs, kicks open the door and yells, "I'm looking for the meanest, roughest, toughest hooker in town."

The woman inside the room looks at the miner and says, "You found her!" Then she strips naked, bends over and grabs her ankles.

"How do you know I want to do you like that?" asks the miner.

"I don't," replies the hooker, "I just thought you might like to open those beers first."

Battle beyond the stars

Luke Skywalker goes to his lightsaber practice with Yoda carrying a spoon.

"What curious object is that?" asks Yoda.

"It's the spoon that I've used since I was a little boy," replies Luke. "I take it everywhere I go and keep it in my shirt pocket at all times."

Unimpressed, Yoda puts Luke through his paces with an intense lightsaber battle and in the heat of the duel Yoda delivers a stinging blow to Luke's chest, but the little green fella's lightsaber strikes Luke's spoon. It shatters, saving the Jedi's life.

That night at dinner in Yoda's hut, Luke is thinking about the loss of his spoon, his most prized possession after his lightsaber.

"Moping stop you," demands Yoda. "My wooden spoon use you; just as good it is."

But Yoda's new spoon just doesn't feel right.

"I'll never be able to eat again!" cries the young Jedi.

Suddenly, Obi-wan appears hovering above his plate.

"Luke," says the Jedi Master. "Use the fork."

Now we are six

A little girl walks into the lounge one Sunday morning where her Dad is reading the paper.

"Where does poo come from?" she asks.

Father, feeling a little perturbed that his five-year-old daughter is already asking difficult questions, thinks for a moment and says:

"Well, you know we just ate breakfast?"

"Yes," replies the girl.

"Well, the food goes into our tummies and our bodies take out all the good stuff, and then whatever's left over comes out of our bottoms when we go to the toilet. That's poo."

The little girl looks perplexed and stares at him in stunned silence for a few seconds before asking: "And Tigger?"

The finer things

A man finds a genie in a bottle and is offered three wishes. First he asks for a fast sports car. Suddenly, a Ferrari appears before him. Next, he asks for a big house. Suddenly, he's sitting in a huge mansion. Finally, he asks to be made irresistible to women. Suddenly, he turns into a box of luxury chocolates.

Driving me nuts

A tour bus driver is driving with a bus load of OAPs when he is tapped on his shoulder by a little old lady. She offers him a handful of peanuts, which he gratefully munches up. After about 15 minutes, she taps him on his shoulder again and she hands him another handful of peanuts.

When she is about to hand him yet another batch he asks her: "Why don`t you eat the peanuts yourself?"

"We can't chew them because we've no teeth," she replies. "We just love the chocolate around them."

Flying rats

The Mayor of London is worried because pigeon crap is ruining the streets and it's costing a fortune to keep them clean.

One day a man arrives at the London Assembly building and offers the Mayor a proposition: "I can rid your beautiful city of its plague of pigeons without cost to the city, but you must promise not to ask me any questions. Or you can pay me £5 million and ask one question." The Mayor considers the offer and accepts.

Next day the man climbs to the top of the London Assembly building, opens his coat and releases a blue pigeon that flies up into the sky. All the pigeons in London see it and they follow it out of the city. The next day the blue pigeon returns completely alone to the man and the Mayor is suitably impressed.

Even though the pigeon-fancier charges nothing, the Mayor presents him with a cheque for five million quid.

"You have done the city and the people of London a wonderful service," he declares, "but I have paid you five million pounds so that I can ask you one question."

"Fire away," says the man.

"By any chance, do you know where we can find a blue Australian?" the Mayor asks.

The perfect gift

Two friends are sitting at a bar shooting the breeze over a couple of jars.

"I got my wife a diamond ring for her birthday," says one guy.

"Didn't you tell me she wanted an SUV?" asks his pal.

"Yeah, but I couldn't find a fake Range Rover."

Bad decision

A Ukrainian woman bumps into the Chelsea football squad in a nightclub. She approaches John Terry and asks for his autograph on her breast. Terry agrees and she obliges by lifting up her top so that he can sign her left one. She then asks Drogba for his autograph on her other breast. Drogba willingly agrees and she obliges by lifting up her top so he can sign the right one. She then asks Mourinho for his autograph somewhere a bit more private. Jose agrees and the woman obliges by dropping her knickers. Suddenly, Mourinho turns white and says, "On second thoughts, I think I'll pass. The last time I signed a Ukrainian twat it cost me £30 million."

How do you make Robbie Savage go woof?
Douse him in petrol and set light to him.

Intimate strangers

One day at a bus stop there's a girl wearing a skin-tight miniskirt.

Just as she's about to get on the bus she realises that her skirt is so tight she can't lift her foot high enough to reach the first step.

Thinking it will give her enough slack to raise her leg, she reaches back and unzips her skirt a little. However, she can't reach the step, so she reaches back once again to unzip it a little more, but still she can't reach the step. So, with her skirt zipper halfway down, she reaches back and unzips her skirt all the way. Thinking that she can get on the step now, she lifts up her leg, only to realize it's still impossible.

Seeing how embarrassed the girl is, the man standing behind her puts his hands around her waist and lifts her up on to the first step of the bus. The girl turns around furiously and screams, "How dare you touch me that way? I don't even know you!"

Shocked, the man says, "Well, after you reached around and unzipped my fly three times, I figured that we were friends."

A breed apart

A young entrepreneur starts his own business. He is shrewd and diligent, so business keeps coming in. Pretty soon he realises that he needs an in-house counsel and so he begins interviewing young lawyers.

"As I'm sure you can understand," he starts off with one of the first applicants, "in a business like this, our personal integrity must be beyond question." He leans forward. "Mr Peterson, are you an 'honest' lawyer?"

"Honest?" replies the job prospect. "Let me tell you something about honesty. I'm so honest that my dad lent me £15,000 for my education and I paid back every penny the minute I completed my very first case."

"Impressive. And what sort of case was that?"

"My father filed a small claims suit against me."

Miracle of science

Bored over the summer, Jonathan Woodgate goes shopping and sees something interesting in the kitchen department of a large store.

"What's that?" he asks.

"A Thermos flask," replies the assistant.

"What does it do?" asks Jonathan.

The assistant tells him it keeps hot things hot and cold things cold. Really impressed, Jonathan buys one and takes it along to his next training session with Real Madrid.

"Here, boys, look at this," he says proudly. "It's a Thermos flask."

The lads are impressed.

"What does it do?" they ask.

"It keeps hot things hot and cold things cold, "says Jonathan.

"And what have you got in it?" asks Raul.

"Two cups of coffee and a choc ice," replies Woodgate.

Personal hygiene

One night, a man rolls over in bed and gives his wife a big, knowing grin. Immediately realising his intentions she says, "Not tonight darling. I have an appointment with the gynaecologist tomorrow morning and I want to stay fresh and clean."

Dejected and disappointed, the man rolls over and tries to get to sleep. A few minutes later he rolls over and prods his wife again.

"Tell me; do you have a dental appointment tomorrow, too?"

Have you heard about the new super-sensitive condoms?
They hang around after the man leaves.

The old enemy

A family of England supporters head out one Saturday to get their new football kits. In the sports shop the son picks up a Scotland football shirt and says to his sister, "I've decided I'm going to be a Scotland supporter."

The sister is outraged at this, promptly whacks him round the head and says, "Go talk to your mother!"

The lad goes off and finds his mother. "Mum, I've decided I'm going to be a Scotland supporter and I want this shirt."

The mother is outraged and promptly whacks him round the head and says, "Go talk to your father."

Off goes the lad again and finds his father. "Dad, I've decided I'm going to be a Scotland supporter and I want this shirt."

The father is outraged, promptly whacks his son round the head and says, "No son of mine is ever going to be seen in that!"

About half an hour later, they're all back in the car heading home. The father turns to the son and says, "Son, I hope you have learned something today?"

The son turns to his dad and says, "Yes, I have."

"Good, son, what is it?" says the dad.

The son replies, "I've only been a Scotland supporter for an hour and I already hate you English bastards!"

Filth commandment

A minister was asked to dinner by one of his parishioners, whom he knew was a slovenly housekeeper. When he sat down at the table, he noticed that the dishes were the dirtiest that he had ever seen in his life.

"Were these dishes ever washed?" he asked his hostess, running his fingers over the grit and grime.

She replied, "They're as clean as soap and water could get them."

He felt a bit apprehensive, but blessed the food anyway and started eating. It was really delicious and he said so, despite the dirty dishes.

When dinner was over, the hostess took the dishes outside and yelled, to her dogs "Here, Soap! Here, Water!"

Slow learner

One morning four golfers are waiting at the men's tee, while a foursome of ladies are hitting from the ladies' tee. The ladies take their time, but finally the last woman is ready to tee off. She hacks it about 10 feet, curses, walks over to the ball and hacks it another 10 feet.

She looks up at the watching men, shrugs and says, "I guess all those f**king lessons I took this winter didn't help."

One of the guys replies, "Now there's your problem. You should've taken golf lessons instead. Still, d'ya fancy a drink?"

What's the ultimate rejection?
You're masturbating and your hand falls asleep.

Blame game

While out for a drive, an elderly couple stop at a service station for lunch. Back on the road afterwards, the elderly woman realises that she's left her glasses in the service station.

By then, they've travelled quite a distance and have to go even further before they can find a place to turn around.

The old fella moans and complains all the way back to the restaurant. He calls his wife every name he can think of and when they finally arrive back at the service station, and the woman gets out of the car to retrieve her glasses, the man yells to her, "And while you're in there, you might as well get my wallet, too!"

What do you get when a grenade is thrown into a French kitchen?

Linoleum Blownapart.

Man and superman

A big city promoter hears of a man who has 20 wives who he makes love to every day. Impressed, the promoter hires the man to exhibit his prowess on stage in London's West End. On opening night it all goes wrong, when the man makes love to only ten of his wives before he collapses with exhaustion.

The curtain falls and the promoter rushes up to his failed investment. "What happened?" he asks.

"I don't know," the man answers. "Everything went fine in rehearsal!"

The first cuckold of spring

A guy comes home from work, walks into his bedroom and finds a stranger making love to his wife. He says, "What the hell are you two doing?"

His wife turns to the stranger and says, "I told you he was stupid."

Down, boy

Two men walking down the road see a dog licking its balls.

The first man says, "I wish I could do that."

The second man replies, "Better stroke him first – he might bite."

All that kneeling

A drunk man sits down on a train seat next to a priest. The man's tie is stained, his face is plastered with red lipstick and a half-empty bottle of gin is sticking out of his torn coat pocket. He opens his newspaper and begins reading.

After a few minutes the man turns to the priest and asks, "Say, Father, what causes arthritis?"

"My Son, it's caused by loose living, sleeping with wanton women, drinking too much alcohol and having contempt for your fellow man," the priest replies.

"Well, I'll be damned," the drunk mutters, returning to his paper.

The priest, thinking about what he said, nudges the man and apologises. "I'm very sorry. I didn't mean to come on so strong. How long have you had arthritis?"

"I don't, Father," the man says. "I was just reading here that the Pope does."

Upscale dining

A man walks into a Japanese restaurant with his wife. The waiter approaches and the man asks for a table for two. As they are waiting for a table to be prepared, his wife notices a tank full of beautiful tropical fish.

The wife turns to her husband and says that she wants the same fish for a tank at home. The husband agrees and asks the waiter what the fish are called.

The waiter replies, "Sushi, sir."

Plastered again

Mike staggers home very late after another late night drinking session with his best mates and removes his shoes to avoid waking his missus. He tiptoes as quietly as he can towards the stairs, but trips and knocks a vase on to the floor, which he then falls on to, cutting his buttocks. Managing not to shout, he stands up and pulls his pants down to examine the damage in the hall mirror. His backside is cut and bleeding, so he grabs a box of plasters and sticks them wherever he can see blood. He then hides the almost empty plaster box and stumbles into bed.

The next morning, Mike awakes with searing pain in both his head and arse, to see his wife staring at him.

"You were drunk again last night, weren't you?" she says.

"Why would you say such a mean thing?" he asks.

"Well," she says, "it could be the open front door. Or the broken glass at the bottom of the stairs. Or the drops of blood on the stairs. It could even be your bloodshot eyes, but mostly, it's all those bloody plasters stuck to the hall mirror!"

The pits

After a particularly gruelling F1 race, Flavio Briatore is sitting on his luxury yacht in Monaco harbour sipping some white wine. On the TV is a documentary about how unemployed youths from Liverpool can remove a set of wheels in less than six seconds with no proper equipment.

Flavio is amazed by this and immediately fires Renault's entire pit crew, who can only do it in eight seconds with millions of Euros-worth of high-tech equipment at their disposal. Taking advantage of one of Tony Blair's youth opportunity schemes, Flavio fills the vacant places in Renault's garage with the youths from the documentary.

At the crew's first practice the racing bigwig is amazed as the young Scousers successfully change the tyres of Giancarlo Fisichella's car in less than six seconds, and he walks away confident that Renault will take the F1 crown again this season.

Suddenly, his mobile phone rings. It's Briatore's boss, the President of Renault.

"Have you seen those new guys in the pit?" brags Briatore. "No one can stop us this year. It only took them six seconds to change the tyres."

"You idiot!" comes the reply from the company president. "Within 12 seconds they'd resprayed, rebadged and sold the car to Red Bull for eight bottles of Heineken and some photos of David Coulthard's bird in the shower!"

Where would you be without a sense of humour? Germany.

Answer that!

God is sitting in Heaven when a scientist says to him, "Lord, we don't need you any more. Science has finally figured out a way to create life out of nothing. We can now do what you did in the beginning."

"Oh, is that so? Tell me," replies God.

"Well," says the scientist, "we can take dirt and breathe life into it, thus creating man."

"Well, that's interesting. Show me," booms God.

So the scientist bends down to the earth and starts to breathe on the soil.

"Oi!" says God. "Get your own dirt."

What's the difference between a car mechanic and a herd of rhinos?
The mechanic charges more.

Kiss of life

A woman has been in a coma for several weeks, but one day nurses notice a slight response while washing her private parts. They rush to her husband and explain the surprise, suggesting a little oral sex might bring her round, to which he readily agrees. A few minutes later her monitor flatlines, showing no pulse or heart rate.

The nurses rush into the room crying, "What happened!?"

"I'm not sure," the husband replies sadly. "She may have choked."

Johnny cash

An English tourist walks into a New York drugstore and asks for a packet of condoms.

"Rubbers, eh?" says the chemist, recognising his customer is English. "That'll be ten dollars, including the tax."

"Jesus!" cries the Englishman. "Back home we just roll them on."

The beautiful game

Halfway through the first half of a school football game, the coach calls one of his nine-year-old players aside and asks, "Do you understand what co-operation is? What a team is?"

The little boy nods in the affirmative.

"Do you understand that what matters is whether we win or lose together as a team?" demands the coach.

The little boy nods.

"So," the coach continues, "I'm sure you know, when you're called offside, you shouldn't argue, swear, attack the ref or call him an idiot. Do you understand all that?"

Again the little boy nods.

The coach continues, "And when I take you off so another boy gets a chance to play, it's not good sportsmanship to call your coach a tw*t, is it?"

Again the little boy agrees.

"Good," says the coach. "Now go over there and explain all that to your dad."

Who was the last person to box Rocky Marciano? His undertaker.

Learning curve

While making his rounds, a doctor points out an X-ray to a group of medical students.

"As you can see," he says, "the patient limps because his left fibula and tibia are radically arched."

The doctor turns to one of the students and asks, "What would you do in a case like this?"

"Well," ponders the student, "I suppose I'd limp, too."

Square meal

Two men went into a pub, ordered two beers, took some sandwiches out of their packs and started to eat them.

"You can't eat your own sandwiches in here," complained the pub-owner.

The two men stopped, looked at each other and then swapped their sandwiches.

What's the difference between an Argentine football fan and a bad cup of coffee?
Nothing; they're both bitter.

Cry for help

Last night police were called to a branch of Pizza Hut after the body of a member of staff was found covered in mushrooms, onions, ham and cheese. The police spokesman said that there was a strong possibility that the man had topped himself.

How do you convince Jade Goody to go to bed with you?
Piece of cake.

Applied psychology

A man bought a new fridge for his house. To get rid of his old fridge, he put it in the driveway and hung a sign on it saying: "Free to good home. You want it, you take it."

For three days the fridge sat there without even one person looking twice at it.

He eventually decided that people were too suspicious. It looked too good to be true. He changed the sign to read: "Fridge for sale, £50."

The next day someone stole it.

Safe pair of hands

Two young travellers are braving their way across Mexico behind the wheel of an old van, when they come across a group of bandits standing behind a roadblock.

The head honcho walks around to the door, sticks a gun into their faces and says, "Start masturbating, gringos!"

Shocked but fearing for their lives, the pair duly oblige – and, despite the stress, manage to perform. As soon as they've finished the bandit chief leans in and demands "Again!"

They manage a repeat performance, but are then told to continue until, tired and sore, the pair are physically incapable of another erection.

"Good work," smiles the toothless Mexican as a dark figure emerges from the trees. "Now drive my sister into town."

Nuts

> How many Manchester City fans does it take to change a lightbulb?
> None. They're quite happy living in the shadows.

Holey communion

An old couple are sitting in church. After listening to the priest's sermon the old lady says to her husband, "I've just done a silent fart; what should I do?"

The old man replies: "Turn your bloody hearing aid up!"

Plain speaking

At one American university, students in the psychology class are attending their first lecture on emotional extremes.

"Just to establish some parameters," says the professor to a student from Arkansas, "what is the opposite of joy?"

"Sadness," replies the diligent student.

"And the opposite of depression?" he asks of a young lady from Oklahoma.

"Elation," she says.

"And you, sir," he says to a young man from Texas, "what about the opposite of woe?"

The Texan replies, "Sir, I believe that would be 'giddy up.'"

A view to a quill

What's the difference between a porcupine and a pop star's tour bus?

The porcupine has the pricks on the outside.

A good man is hard to find

A middle-aged man and woman meet, fall in love and decide to get married. On their wedding night they settle into the bridal suite at their hotel and the bride says to her new groom, "Please promise to be gentle; I'm still a virgin."

The startled groom says, "How can that be? You've been married three times before."

The bride responds, "Well, you see, my first husband was a psychiatrist and all he ever wanted to do was talk about it.

"My second husband was a gynaecologist and all he ever wanted to do was look at it.

"And my third husband was a stamp collector and all he ever wanted to do was... God, I miss him!"

Bust-up

"My God! What happened to you?" the bartender asks Jim as he hobbles in on a crutch, one arm in a cast.

"I got in a fight with Steve Riley," he replies.

"Riley? He's your best mate and about half the size of you," the bartender says. "He must have had a weapon in his hand."

"Yeah. He had a shovel."

"Dear Lord. Didn't you have anything in your hands?"

"His wife's tits," Jim laments. "They're beautiful, but not much use in a fight."

Two flies are in an airing cupboard. Which one's in the army?
The one on the tank.

Bodily resurrection

A middle-aged woman has a heart attack and is taken to the hospital. While on the operating table she has a near-death experience. Seeing God, she asks: "Is my time up?"

God says, "No, you have another 43 years, two months and eight days to live."

Upon recovery, the woman decides to stay in the hospital and have a facelift, liposuction and a tummy tuck.

While crossing the street on her way home, she's killed by an ambulance. Arriving in front of God, she demands, "I thought you said I had another 40 years?"

God replies, "I didn't recognise you."

Leaf well alone

Two caterpillars are sitting on a leaf when a butterfly flutters past them.

One caterpillar turns to the other and says, "You'd never get me up in one of those."

There are two cowboys in the kitchen. Which is the real one?
The one on the range.

It's a free country

A man phones up his local building firm and says: "I want a skip outside my house."

"Go ahead; I'm not stopping you," the builder replies.

Double trouble

Two girlfriends are having a conversation about their boyfriends.

The first one says: "My boyfriend said he fantasises about having a threesome."

The other replies, "Yeah; most men do. What did you tell him?"

"I said, 'Why would you want to piss off two women?'"

Lucky escape

Two men are robbing a hotel.

"I hear sirens. Jump!" says the first one.

"But we're on the 13th floor!" his fellow thief replies.

"This is no time to be superstitious!"

Penne for your thoughts

A man and woman go on date to an Italian restaurant. They arrive, order and the woman disappears to the toilet. The man waits for five minutes but there's still no sign of the woman. He is still waiting for her 20 minutes later when the food has arrived.

Finally, after half an hour she eventually comes back to find the man squeezing the pasta on his plate.

"What on earth do you think you are doing!" she screams in disgust.

"I was feeling cannelloni," he replies.

Where your money goes

While flying to South Africa, a plane crashes in desolate mountain terrain. The only survivor is an elderly lady who manages to stumble out of the wreckage. After crawling, hungry and exhausted, for several miles she finds shelter in a cave. After some time a Red Cross search party arrives and begins crossing the mountain range looking for survivors. After a few hours they spot the cave entrance. "Is anyone alive in there?" shouts the group leader.

"Who's that?" shouts the old lady.

"Red Cross!" answers the leader.

"Jesus, you guys get everywhere!" shouts the old dear. "I've already donated."

Bloody nuisance

Two nuns are driving down a road late at night when a vampire jumps on to the bonnet.

The nun who is driving says to the other, "Quick! Show him your cross."

So the other nun leans out of the window and shouts, "Get off our f*cking car!"

Quick thinking

Resolving to surprise her husband, an executive's wife stops by his office. When she opens the door, she finds him with his secretary sitting in his lap.

Without hesitating, he dictates, "…and in conclusion, gentlemen, budget cuts or no budget cuts, I cannot continue to operate this office with just one chair."

> **What should you do if a Rottweiler starts shagging your leg?**
> **Fake an orgasm.**

My heart won't go on

A Liverpool fan, a Man U fan and a Chelsea fan find themselves waiting outside the pearly gates.

Eventually, St Peter emerges and informs them that in order to get into heaven, they'll each have to answer one question. St Peter turns to the Scouser first.

"What was the name of the ship that crashed into the iceberg? They made a movie about it."

The Liverpudlian answers quickly, "That would be Titanic."

St Peter lets him through the gates.

He then turns to the United supporter and asks: "How many people died on the ship?" Fortunately, the Manc has just seen the DVD.

"1,228," he answers.

"That's right! You may enter."

St Peter then turns to the Chelsea fan. "Name them."

In greatest need

A man walks into a chemist and asks for a bottle of Viagra. The pharmacist eyes him suspiciously. "Do you have a prescription for that?" he asks.

"No," says the man, "but will this picture of my wife do?"

Chump, chomp, champ

A Russian and an American wrestler make it to the final at the Olympics. Before the pair contest the gold medal, the American wrestler's trainer comes up to him and says, "Now, don't forget all the research we've done on this Russian. He's never lost a match because of this 'pretzel' hold he has. Whatever you do, don't let him get you in this hold! If he does, you're finished!"

The wrestler nods in agreement. As the match begins, the American and the Russian circle each other several times looking for an opening. All of a sudden the Russian lunges forward, grabs the American and wraps him up in the dreaded pretzel hold.

A sigh of disappointment goes up from the crowd, and the trainer buries his face in his hands.

Suddenly there is a horrible scream and the crowd cheers. The trainer raises his head just in time to see the Russian flying up in the air. The Russian's back hits the mat with a thud and the American weakly collapses on top of him, gets the pin and wins the match.

The trainer is astounded. When he finally gets the American wrestler alone, he asks, "How did you ever get out of that hold? No one has ever done it before!"

The wrestler answers, "Well, I was ready to give up when he got me in that hold, but at the last moment I opened my eyes and saw this pair of balls right in front of my face. I thought

I had nothing to lose, so with my last ounce of strength I stretched out my neck and bit those babies just as hard as I could. You'd be amazed how strong you get when you bite your own balls!"

Only trying to help

One winter morning an old couple, Norman and Sarah, are listening to the radio over breakfast. The announcer says, "We're going to have eight to ten inches of snow today. You must park your car on the even-numbered side of the street, so the snow ploughs can get through."

Norman's wife goes out and moves her car.

A week later while they are eating breakfast, the radio announcer says, "We're expecting ten to 12 inches of snow today. You must park your car on the odd-numbered side of the street, so the snow ploughs can get through."

Norman's wife dutifully goes out and moves her car again.

The next week again they're having breakfast, when the radio announcer says: "We're expecting 12 to 14 inches of snow today. You must park..." Then the power goes out. Norman's wife is very upset and with a worried look on her face she says, "Honey, I don't know what to do. Which side of the street do I need to park on so the snow plough can get through?"

With love and understanding in his voice, Norman says, "Why don't you just leave it in the garage this time, dear?"

What do you call a hippy's wife?
Mississippi.

Miracles take a little longer

A man walking along a beach is deep in prayer. Suddenly, the sky clouds over and in a booming voice the Lord says, "Because you have been so faithful to me, I will grant you one wish."

The man says, "Build a bridge from my home in Manchester to the Greek islands, so whenever I want a holiday I can just drive there."

The Lord says, "Your request is very selfish. Think of the supports required to reach the bottom of the sea; the concrete and steel it would take; the destruction to the environment; and the havoc caused to shipping lanes. Your bridge will nearly exhaust all of the world's natural resources. Take a little more time and think of something else."

The man says: "OK Lord, you're right, I'm sorry I was thoughless. I wish I could understand my wife; how she feels inside; why she cries."

The Lord replies, "So, do you want two lanes or four on that bridge, then?"

Banned substances

The ambitious coach of a girls' athletics team starts giving his squad steroids. Their performance soars, and they go on to win the county and national championships. The day after the nationals, Penelope, a 16-year-old hurdler, comes into his office.

"I have a problem," she says, "Hair's starting to grow on my chest."

"Oh my God!" yells the coach. "How far down does it go?"

"Down to my balls," she replies.

What's the biggest crime committed by transvestites?
Male fraud.

Shall we gather at the river?

A drunk is stumbling through the woods when he comes across a preacher baptising people in the river. He walks down to the water's edge, then trips and falls before the holy man.

Almost overcome by the smell of alcohol, the preacher pipes up: "Lord have mercy on your drunken soul, brother; are you ready to find Jesus?"

Out of his skull, the drunk agrees: "Yes, I am!"

And with that, the preacher grabs him and dunks him under the water.

Moments later, he drags the boozer back up: "Brother, have you found Jesus?"

"No, preacher," stammers the drunk, "I have not!"

Stunned by this, the preacher sends the drunk down again… this time leaving him a little longer.

Finally he drags him back up again: "Rid your soul of the poison, brother; have you found Jesus?"

Gasping for air, the drunk splutters a reply: "No, preacher; I have not!"

At his wits' end, the preacher sends the drunk down one last time.

A full minute later, he pulls him out: "For the love of God," shouts the preacher, "tell me you've found Jesus!"

Coughing his lungs up, the drunk wipes his eyes and turns to the preacher: "You sure this is where he fell in?"

Getting results

A man calls a local hospital.

"Hello. Could you connect me to the person who gives information about patients? I'd like to find out if a patient is getting better, doing as expected or getting worse," he says.

The voice on the other end says, "What is the patient's name and room number?"

"Brian Johnson, room 302," says the man.

"I'll connect you with the nursing station," says the receptionist.

After a brief pause, the man hears: "3-A Nursing Station. How can I help you?"

"I'd like to know the condition of Brian Johnson in room 302," says the man.

"Just a moment. Let me look at his records… Mr Johnson is doing very well. In fact, he's had two full meals, his blood pressure is fine, he's to be taken off the heart monitor in a couple of hours and, if he continues this improvement, Dr Cohen is going to send him home Tuesday at noon."

The man says, "What a relief! Oh, that's fantastic… that's wonderful news!"

The nurse says, "Are you are a family member or a close friend?"

"Neither! I'm Brian Johnson in 302! Nobody here tells me jack shit."

What did the sign in the vet's waiting room say? Sit! Stay!

My body is a temple

A woman walked up to an old man sitting in a chair on his porch. "I couldn't help but notice how happy you look," she said. "What's your secret for a long, happy life?"

"I smoke three packs a day, drink a case of beer, eat fatty foods and never, ever exercise," he replied.

"Wow; that's amazing," she said, "How old are you?"

"Twenty-six."

Fowl language

A young man's mother is now retired and living in Miami Beach. He doesn't see her that often. His father is no longer around and he is worried that his mum is lonely. For her birthday, he purchases a rare parrot, trained to speak seven languages. He has a courier deliver the bird to his dear old mother. A few days later, he calls to see that she got the bird. "Mum, what do you think of the parrot?"

"It was a little tough, actually. I should have cooked it longer," says the old dear.

"You ate the bird? Mum, that bird was really expensive. It spoke seven languages!" says the horrified son.

"Oh, excuse me! If the bird was so damn smart, why didn't it say something when I put it in the oven?"

Left high and dry

A large cup and two smaller ones go out for a meal at a posh restaurant. When the bill arrives, the small cups do a runner, leaving their pal to pay up.

A week later, the three are back and, once again, the large cup is left behind to settle the bill.

The waiter comes up to him, and says, "No offence, mate, but I think your two pals are taking you for a mug."

Lovers' guide

Little Johnny walks past his parents' room one night and sees them making love. Puzzled, he asks his father about it the next morning. "Why were you doing that to mummy last night?"

His father replies, "Because mummy wants a baby."

The next night, Johnny spots mummy giving daddy a blowjob and the next morning he asks his father, "Why was mummy doing that to you last night?"

His father replies, "Because mummy wants a BMW."

Between ourselves

A man is staying at a hotel on a business trip and, feeling lonely, reaches for an escort girl's business card he'd taken from a phone box earlier. He rings the number and a sexy-sounding woman picks up the phone and says, "Hello?"

"Hello," he says. "I hear you give a great massage and I'd like you to come to my hotel room to give me one… No, wait. I'll be straight with you. I'm all alone and all I want is sex – and I'm talking some seriously kinky stuff. Whips, chains, the lot – how does that sound?"

"That sounds fair enough," says the woman, "but for an outside line you need to dial 9."

Sense of perspective

A very successful lawyer parks his brand-new BMW in front of the office, ready to show it off to his colleagues. As he gets out, a truck comes along, too close to the kerb, and completely tears off the Beemer's driver's door.

The lawyer immediately grabs his mobile, dials 999, and in about five minutes a police car turns up. Before the cop has a chance to ask any questions, the lawyer starts screaming hysterically. The BMW, which he'd just picked up the day before, is now completely ruined and will never be the same, no matter how the body shop tries to make it new again.

After the lawyer finally winds down from his rant, the cop shakes his head in disgust. "I can't believe how materialistic you lawyers are," he says. "You're so focused on your possessions that you neglect the most important things in life."

"How can you say such a thing?" asks the lawyer.

The cop replies, "You sick sod; don't you even realise that your left arm's missing? It got ripped off when the truck hit you!"

"My God!" screams the lawyer. "Where's my Rolex?"

> What do you get if you mix holy water with a laxative?
> A religious movement.

Saving himself

David Beckham walks into a pub. The landlord says, "Your usual, David?"

Beckham replies, "Yeah. Just a half, then I'm off."

It's a miracle!

An alien is visiting earth to research the local customs. After a while he returns to the mothership to share his knowledge with the other aliens. He gathers his fellow ETs and tells of how he landed in a green and pleasant land called England and witnessed a religious ceremony.

"I went to a large green field shaped like a meteorite crater. Around the edges there were several thousand worshippers. Two priests walked to the centre of the field to a rectangular area and hammered six spears into the ground, three at each end. Then eleven more priests walked out, clad in white robes. Then two high priests wielding clubs walked to the centre and one of the other priests started throwing a red orb at the ones with the clubs."

"Ooooh," replies the amazed alien throng collectively, "what happened next?"

"Well," says the explorer alien. "Then it began to rain."

The greatest show on Earth

Why is marriage like a three-ring circus?

First there's the engagement ring, then there's the wedding ring, and then comes the suffering.

Lady Luck

A very attractive blonde arrives at a casino and bets £20,000 on a single roll of the dice.

"I hope you don't mind," she says, "but I feel much luckier when I'm completely naked."

With that, she strips off, bends over the table slowly and rolls the dice. Then she yells out, "Yes! I've won! I've won!" She

jumps up and down, hugs each of the dealers, scoops up all the chips on the table along with her clothes, and then quickly departs.

The dealers stare at each other utterly dumbfounded.

Finally, one of them asks, "So, what did she roll?"

"No idea," replies the other. "I thought you were watching."

How do you stop a snake from striking?
Pay it decent wages.

Holy orders

At the Gates of Heaven, God decides to put in a personal appearance and says, "I want the men to make two lines: one line for the men who were true heads of their households and the other line for the men who were dominated by their women. I want all the women to report to St Peter."

Soon, the women are gone and there are two lines of men. The line of men who were dominated by their wives is 100 miles long, and in the line of men who truly were heads of their household, there is only one man.

God said, "You men should be ashamed of yourselves. I created you to be the head of your household. You have been disobedient and not fulfilled your purpose. I told you to be the spiritual leader in your family. Of all of you, only one obeyed. Learn from him! Tell them, my son, how did you manage to be the only one in this line?"

The man replies, "I don't know. My wife told me to stand here."

In the mean time

Two old Englishmen and two old Irishmen enter a bar and see a sign that reads, "Old Timers' Bar: All Drinks 50p!"

When the old bartender spots them he calls out: "Come on in and let me pour you a drink! What'll it be?"

The four men each ask for a martini and the bartender duly serves them up and says: "That'll be 50p each, please."

They pay for their drinks, down them and order another round. Again, four excellent martinis are produced for just 50p each.

The old men pay up, but their curiosity is too much and one of the Irishmen asks, "How can you afford to serve martinis as good as these for just 50p a piece?"

"Here's my story," the barman says. "I used to be a tailor in London, but I always wanted to own a bar. Last year I hit the lottery for £15 million and decided to open this place. I think our culture is far too disrespectful to its senior members, so every drink costs 50p: wine, whiskey, beer, anything. Guys like you are coming from all over – it's great."

"Wow! That's quite a story," says one of the Englishmen.

The four of them continue drinking and can't help but notice three other blokes at the end of the bar who don't have a drink between them. In fact, they haven't ordered anything the whole time they've been there.

The Englishman gestures at the men and asks the generous landlord, "What's with them?"

The bartender says, "They're from Scotland. They're waiting for Happy Hour."

> **Why did the Cornishman plant Cheerios in his backyard?**
> **He thought they were doughnut seeds.**

Payment in kind

A wife, frustrated by her husband's bone-idleness around the house in the DIY department, sees cause for concern one day when the toilet clogs up. She decides to ask if he'd mind seeing to it, and is greeted with a gruff, "What, do I look like a toilet cleaner?"

The next day the waste disposal unit seizes up. Summoning all her courage she says, "Sorry to bother you, dear. The waste disposal's broken – would you try to fix it for me?"

"What, do I look like a plumber? Get me a beer and sod off!" is the reply.

To cap it all, the next day the washing machine goes on the blink and, taking her life in her hands, the wife addresses the sofa-bound slob: "Darling, I know you're busy, but the washing machine's packed up."

"What, do I look like a bloody washing machine repairman?" her old man says.

Finally, fed up, she calls out three different repairmen to come and fix her appliances.

That evening, she informs her husband of this. He frowns angrily and asks, "So how much will it cost?"

"Well, they said I could pay them either by baking a cake or screwing them all," she says.

"What type of cake did they want?" he growls.

"What, do I look like Delia Smith?" she replies.

A first time for everything

A linguistics professor is lecturing his class.

"In English," he says, "a double negative forms a positive. However, in some languages, such as Russian, a double negative remains a negative. But there isn't a single language, not one, in which a double positive can express a negative."

A sarcastic voice from the back of the room replies, "Yeah: right."

Empathy

A priest, a doctor and a lawyer are waiting one morning on a particularly slow group of golfers.

"What's wrong with these guys?" fumes the lawyer. "We must have been waiting for 15 minutes!"

"I don't know," says the doctor, "but I've never seen such ineptitude!"

"Here comes the greenskeeper," says the priest. "Let's have a word with him. Say, George, what's with that group ahead of us? They're rather slow, aren't they?"

"Oh, yes," says George, "That's the group of blind firemen. They lost their sight while saving our club last year. We let them play here any time free of charge!"

Everyone is silent for a moment.

Then the priest says, "That's so sad, I think I'll say a prayer for them tonight."

"And I'm going to contact my ophthalmologist buddy and see if there's anything he can do for them," the doctor adds.

"Why can't the selfish bastards damn well play at night?" asks the lawyer.

Frank confession

A young woman on a flight from New York to London asks the priest sitting beside her, "Father, may I ask a favour?"

"Of course, my child. What may I do for you?"

"Well, I bought an expensive woman's electronic hair dryer for my mother's birthday," says the female passenger. "The dryer is unopened and well over the Customs limits, and I'm afraid they'll confiscate it. Is there any way you could carry it through Customs for me? Under your robes perhaps?"

"I would love to help you, my dear," says the man of the cloth, "but I must warn you: I will not lie."

"With your honest face, Father, no one will question you," replies the woman.

When they reach the Customs area, the women lets the priest go ahead of her. The Customs official asks, "Father, do you have anything to declare?"

"From the top of my head down to my waist, I have nothing to declare," answers the priest.

"And what do you have to declare from your waist to the floor?" says the official.

"I have a marvellous instrument designed to be used on a woman, but which is, to date, unused."

Roaring with laughter, the official says, "Go ahead, Father. Next."

Why does Rupert the Bear wear checked trousers? Because he doesn't have any fashion sense.

Baring their souls

While redecorating a church, three nuns become extremely hot and sweaty in their habits, so Mother Superior says, "Let's take our clothes off and work naked."

The other two nuns disapprove and ask, "What if someone sees us?"

But the Mother Superior says, "Don't worry; no one will see us. We'll just lock the door."

So the other nuns agree, strip down and return to work.

Suddenly, they hear a knock at the door and grab their clothes in a panic.

Mother Superior runs to the door and calls through, "Who is it?"

"Blind man," a man's voice comes back.

So she opens the door and lets in the blind man. He turns to the nuns and says, "Great tits, ladies. Now, where do you want these blinds?"

Chance in a vermilion

A sailor is driven off course by a storm and smashes into a small island. The next morning, he awakes on the beach. The sand and sky are reddish. Walking around in a daze, the sailor sees red birds, red grass, red trees and red bananas. He is shocked to find that even his skin is red.

"Oh, no!" he exclaims. "I'm marooned!"

Crime of the century

A tortoise is ambling down an alleyway when he's mugged by a gang of snails. A police detective comes to investigate and asks the turtle if he can explain what happened. The tortoise looks at the detective with a confused look on his face and replies: "I don't know; it all happened so fast."

Sahara dessert

A man crawls out of the desert and into a small village, which has some market stalls in the street.

He crawls up to the first one. "Water, water! Give me water!" he cries.

"I'm sorry," says the first stallholder, "I only sell custard."

The man crawls up to the second stall. "Water, water! Give me water!" he cries.

"I'm sorry," says the second stallholder, "I only sell cream and sponge."

The man then crawls up to a third stall. "Water, water! Give me water!" he cries.

"I'm sorry," says the third stallholder, "I only sell hundreds and thousands."

"I can't believe no one has any water," says the parched man.

"I know," says the stallholder, "it is a trifle bazaar."

What is the height of optimism?
An English batsman applying sunscreen.

Wins... or not

A man is walking through the Sahara desert, desperate for water, when he sees something far off in the distance. Hoping to find water, he walks towards the image, only to find a little old man sitting at a card table with a bunch of neckties laid out on it. The man asks, "Please, I'm dying of thirst; can I have some water?"

The man replies, "I don't have any water, but why don't you buy a tie? Here's one that goes nicely with your ripped clothes."

The young guy shouts, "I don't want a tie, you idiot, I need water!"

"OK, don't buy a tie. But to show you what a nice guy I am, I'll tell you that over that hill there, about four miles, is a nice restaurant. Walk that way; they'll give you all the water you want."

The man thanks him and walks away towards the hill and eventually disappears. Three hours later he comes crawling back to where the man is sitting behind his card table. He says, "I told you: about four miles over that hill. Couldn't you find it?"

The young fella rasps, "I found it all right. They wouldn't let me in without a tie."

What do you call a dog with brass balls and no hind legs?

Sparky.

142

Entrepreneur

The kids filed back into class Monday morning. Their weekend assignment was to sell something, then give a talk on salesmanship.

Little Mary led off. "I sold homemade biscuits and I made £30," she said proudly.

"Very good," said the teacher.

Little Sally was next. "I sold old magazines," she said, "I made £45."

"Very good, Sally," said the teacher.

Eventually, it was Little Mikey's turn. He walked to the front of the classroom and dumped a box full of cash on the teacher's desk. "£2,467," he said.

"How much!" cried the teacher, "What in the world were you selling?"

"Toothbrushes," said Little Mikey.

"Toothbrushes?" echoed the teacher, "How could you possibly sell enough toothbrushes to make that much money?"

"I found the busiest corner in town," said Little Mikey, "I set up a Dip & Chip stand. I gave everybody who walked by a free sample. They all said the same thing. 'Hey! This tastes just like dogsh*t!' Then I'd say, 'It is dogsh*t. Wanna buy a toothbrush?'"

In a class of its own

During the Ryder Cup in Ireland, Tiger Woods drives his
BMW into a petrol station in a remote part of the Irish
countryside. The aged attendant at the pump greets him and is
completely unaware of who the golfing legend is.

"Hello, sir," says the attendant.

Tiger nods a quick hello and bends forward to pick up the
pump.

As he does so, two tees fall out of his shirt pocket on to the
ground.

"What are they, then, son?" asks the attendant.

"They're called tees," replies Tiger.

"Well, what on earth are they for?" inquires the Irishman.

"They're for resting my balls on when I'm driving," says Tiger.

"Fantastic," says the Irishman, "Those BMW boys think of
everything!"

Did you hear about the flasher who was thinking of
retiring?
He decided to stick it out for one more year.

Tail-ender

A guy goes into a doctor's surgery.

"Doctor, I've got a cricket ball stuck up my bum."

The doctor asks, "How's that?"

"Don't you start," the man replies.

Thanks for nothing

A man is walking in the street when he hears a voice. "Stop! Stand still! If you take one more step, a brick will fall on your head and kill you."

The man stops and a big brick falls in front of him. The man is astonished. He walks on and after a while, he's going to cross the road.

Once again, the voice shouts, "Stop! Stand still! If you take one more step, a car will run over you and you will die."

The man does as he's instructed, just as a car comes screeching around the corner, barely missing him.

"Where are you?" The man asks. "Who are you?"

"I am your guardian angel," the voice answers.

"Oh yeah?" the man asks. "And where the hell were you when I bought my Man City season ticket?"

Stain on his character

At the Clintons' one morning, Hillary is reading the papers when she sees a story that Monica Lewinsky turns 31 years old that day. Not being able to resist a dig at her husband, she looks across at Bill over her cornflakes and says, "You know, it says here that Monica Lewinsky is 31 today."

"Oh, really?" replies an awkward Bill.

Not wanting to let her straying husband off the hook just yet, she gives him another dig. "She's certainly grown up fast, hasn't she, Bill?"

"Yes," says Bill, shooting her an irritated glance. "It seems like only yesterday she was crawling around the White House on her hands and knees."

What do you say if someone tries to steal your gate?
Nothing; he might take a fence.

Doing their bit

Due to a shortage of young men a bear, a pig and a rabbit are summoned for National Service. While waiting for the medical examinations, they all admit they're terrified of being killed.

"I'm ungainly and pink," says the pig. "The enemy will see me a mile off – so I decided to chop off my tail." The rabbit nods sagely – and the bear realises the bunny's ears have been removed.

"I just hope it works," says the rabbit. Mystified, the bear watches as both animals enter the examination room – then return, smiling.

"We're free to go," says the rabbit. "They said a rabbit without ears isn't a proper rabbit and a pig without a curly tail isn't a proper pig!"

He's about to leave with the pig when the bear pipes up.

"Hang on a minute!" he cries. "I'm massive and slow – I'd not last a day in combat."

The other two look at the bear.

"Well," says the rabbit, "your sharp teeth could be useful in combat. You might want them removed…"

Nodding miserably, the bear lies down – and the other animals start kicking his fangs out. Eventually, the dazed bear, blood pouring from his mouth, stumbles through the door. A moment later, he returns.

"Did you get let off?" asks the pig.

"Yesh," splutters the bear, "Apparently I'm too fat."

Apt pupil

A man calls his boss one morning and tells him that he's staying home because he's not feeling well.

"What's the matter?" the boss asks.

"I have a bad case of Anal Glaucoma," the man says in a weak voice.

"What the hell is Anal Glaucoma?"

"I can't see my arse coming into work today."

Set your mind at rest

A doctor has been treating an 80-year-old woman for most of her life. When the doctor retires, the patient's case files are given to a new young doctor. At her first check-up with him he studies the files and is amazed to find a prescription for birth control pills.

"Mrs Smith, do you realise you're taking birth control pills?" says the young doc.

"Yes, they help me sleep at night," says Mrs Smith.

"Mrs Smith, I assure you there is absolutely nothing in these that could possibly help you sleep," he says.

The old dear reaches out and pats the young doctor's knee. "Yes, dear, I know that, but every morning, I grind one up and mix it in the glass of orange juice that my 16-year-old granddaughter drinks and, believe me, it helps me sleep at night."

> **What did the elephant say to the man?**
> **"How do you breathe through that thing?"**

Potty mouth

Snoop Dogg is minding his baby son when, suddenly, the baby gargles, "Mother…"

The doting gangsta rapper is overjoyed and shouts out: "Fo Shizzle! You just said half a word!"

Lower the undercarriage

A jumbo jet is just coming into the airport on its final approach. The pilot comes on the intercom: "This is your Captain. We're on our final descent. I want to thank you for flying with us today and I hope you enjoy your stay."

But he forgets to switch off the intercom. Now the whole plane can hear his conversation from the cockpit.

The co-pilot says to the pilot. "Well skipper, what are you going to do in town?"

Now all ears are listening to this conversation.

"Well," says the skipper, "first I'm going to check into the hotel and have a beer in the bar. Then I'm going take that new stewardess out for supper: you know, the one with the great legs. I'm going to wine and dine her, then take her back to my room for an all-night marathon session."

Everyone on the plane is trying to get a look at the new stewardess. Mortally embarrassed, she runs from the back of the plane to try and get to the cockpit to turn the intercom off. Halfway down the aisle, she trips over an old lady's bag and falls over.

The old lady leans down, pats her shoulder kindly and says: "No need to run, dear. He's going to have a beer first."

Urbi et orbi

The Pope is taken sick and his trusted physician is summoned.

After examining the holy man for over an hour, the doc leaves the papal bedchamber and tells the assembled cardinals: "The bad news is that it's a rare disorder of the testicles. The good news is that all His Holiness has to do to cure himself is to have sex."

The cardinals argue about this diagnosis at length.

Finally they go to the Pope with the doctor and explain the situation.

After some thought, the Pope says, "I agree to this diagnosis, but under four conditions."

"What are the four conditions?" say the amazed cardinals.

"First the girl must be blind, so that she cannot see with whom she is having sex. Second, she must be deaf, so that she cannot hear with whom she is having sex. Third, she must be dumb so that if somehow she figures out with whom she is having sex, she can tell no one."

After another long pause the cardinals ask, "And the fourth condition?"

"She's got to have big tits," replies the Pope.

Immortal memory

An artist is summoned to paint a picture of General Custer's last thoughts on the anniversary of his death. Two weeks later, the artist comes back with a picture of a cow with a hole in it. Through the hole, there are two Indians having sex.

The historical council is not pleased with the picture, so the members ask the artist to explain the meaning of the picture.

The artist says, "It's simple. The meaning is this. 'Holy cow! Look at the f*cking Indians!'"

Wayside pulpit

A priest and vicar from the local parishes are standing by the side of the road holding up a sign that reads, "The end is near! Turn yourself around now before it's too late!"

They plan to hold up the sign to each passing car.

"Leave us alone, you religious nuts!" yells the first driver as he speeds by.

Seconds later the men of God hear screeching tyres and a big splash from around the corner.

"Do you think," says one clergyman to the other, "we should just put up a sign that says 'Bridge out' instead?"

Leafing so soon?

A nun, badly needing to use the toilet, walks into a local club. The place is hopping with music and loud conversation and every once in a while the lights turn off. Each time this happens, the place erupts into cheers. However, when the revellers spy the nun, the room goes dead silent.

"May I please use the ladies'?" the nun asks.

The bartender replies, "Sure, but I should warn you that there's a statue of a naked man in there wearing only a fig leaf."

"Well, in that case I'll just look the other way," says the nun.

After a few minutes the nun reappears and the whole place stops long enough to give the nun a loud round of applause.

The nun walks over to the bartender and says, "I don't understand. Why did they applaud me just because I went to the ladies'?"

"You see," laughs the bartender, "every time that fig leaf on the statue's lifted up, the lights go out."

Evening, officer

A policeman walks over to a parked car and asks the driver if the car is licensed.

"Of course it is," replies the driver.

"Great; I'll have a pint, then."

Green with envy

A Catholic, a Protestant and a Mormon are sitting on a flight, talking about their families.

The Catholic says, "I have ten kids at home and if I had another one I'd have a football team!"

"Well," says the Protestant, "I have 15 kids at home and if I had another one I'd have an American football team."

"Well," says the Mormon, "I have 17 wives at home." He pauses, sipping at his drink. "If I had another one, I'd have a golf course."

Fair point

A blonde was playing Trivial Pursuit one night. When her turn came she rolled the dice and landed on 'Science & Nature'.

Her question was:

"If you are in a vacuum and someone calls your name, can you hear it?"

She thought for a long while and then asked, "Is it on or off?"

Oops...

A woman gets on a bus, and immediately becomes involved in an argument with the driver when he calls her baby ugly. She pays her fare and storms off to get a seat, visibly upset. The man next to her asks "What's the matter, love?"

"It's that bloody driver, I've never been so insulted in all my life," she replies.

"OK," says the man. "You go down there and sort him out. I'll look after the monkey."

Suffering in silence

A pissed-off wife is complaining about her husband spending all his free time in the local boozer, so one night he takes her along with him.

"What'll you have?" he asks.

"Oh, I don't know: the same as you, I suppose," she replies, so the husband orders a couple of whiskies and throws his down in one shot.

His wife watches him, then takes a sip from her glass and immediately spits it out. "Yuck; that's terrible!" she splutters. "I don't know how you can drink this stuff!"

"Well, there you go," cries the husband. "And you think I'm out enjoying myself every night!"

> **How do you tell a male hippo from a female hippo? The male's the one with the remote.**

Rigid with embarassment

Plucking up his courage, a young man goes to a notorious massage parlour for the first time. As he's not sure when to ask for the dirty deed, he lies on the bed, getting more and more aroused.

After a few minutes, the masseuse notices his condition. "Perhaps sir would like some relief?" she says breathlessly.

The man gulps. "Yes please," he stutters.

With that the lady leaves the room.

She returns a full 15 minutes later. "Well," she says, popping her head around the door. "Finished?"

Nor the years condemn

Two men in their nineties have been friends for decades, and after going through the war together they now just meet a few times a week to play cards. One day they're playing together when one of them suddenly puts down his cards. "Listen, don't get mad at me, pal," he says. "I know we've been friends for years, but I realised the other day that I can't remember your name. I'm really embarrassed but my memory is fading fast. Please remind me."

For three minutes the other old fella just glares back at his mate, shaking his head. Finally, he stirs. "Look," he says, "how soon do you need to know?"

Hard to miss

A woman golfer comes running into the clubhouse in pain.

"Christ, what happened?" says the club pro.

"I got stung by a bee between the first and second holes," she replies.

"Hmmm," the pro murmurs. "Sounds like your stance was a little wide."

First things first

A man and his wife walk into a dentist's office. The man says to the dentist, "Doc, I'm in one hell of a hurry! I have two mates sitting out in my car waiting for us to go and play golf, so forget about the anaesthetic and just pull the tooth and be done with it. We have a 10am tee time at the best golf course in town and it's 9:30 already. I don't have time to wait for the anaesthetic to work!"

The dentist thinks to himself, "My goodness; this is a brave man asking to have his tooth pulled without using anything to kill the pain." So the dentist asks him, "Which tooth is it, sir?"

The man turns to his wife and says, "Open your mouth and show him, dear."

Unassailable logic

A rich lawyer is approached by a charity for a donation. The man from the charity is concerned that the lawyer makes over £1,000,000 a year but doesn't give a penny to good causes.

"First of all," says the lawyer, "my mother is sick and dying in the hospital, and it's not covered by insurance. Second, I have five kids through three divorced marriages. Third, my sister's husband suddenly died and she has no one to support her four children."

"I'm terribly sorry," says the charity man. "I feel bad about asking for money."

The lawyer responds, "Yeah; well, if I'm not giving them anything, why should you get any?"

A lot in common

It's a stockbroker's first day in prison and on meeting his psychotic-looking cellmate, the nutter notices how scared the stockbroker looks and decides to put him at ease.

"I'm in for a white-collar crime, too."

"Oh, really?" says the stockbroker, sighing with relief.

"Yes," says the cellmate, "I killed a vicar."

And the winner is...

A Greek and an Italian are arguing about whose culture has contributed most to the world. The Greek guy says, "Well, we have the Parthenon."

"We have the Colosseum," the Italian counters.

"We gave birth to advanced mathematics," the Greek retorts.

"But we built the Roman Empire," the Italian challenges.

Finally the Greek says triumphantly, "We invented sex!"

"That may be true," replies the Italian, "but we introduced it to women."

Conflicting signals

During an interview for a points operator on the railway, the chief engineer asks a job candidate, "What would you do if the Plymouth-to-London was heading north on Track One and the London-to-Plymouth was heading south on Track One?"

"I'd definitely call my brother," the interviewee replies.

"Why on earth would you call your brother?" the chief engineer asks.

"Because he's never seen a train crash before," the applicant replies.

Oh, I *see*....

A keen golfer is taking lessons with a pro. "What should I do?" asks the man.

"Hold the club gently," the pro replies, "just like you'd hold your wife's breast." Taking the advice, he swings and blasts the ball 250 yards up the fairway.

Ecstatic, the man rushes home to tell his wife the good news. Upon hearing of his success, she books a lesson herself.

The next day the pro watches her swing and says, "No, no, no; you're gripping the club way too hard."

"What can I do?" asked the wife.

"Hold the club gently, just like you'd hold your husband's penis."

The wife listens carefully to the pro's advice, takes a swing, and the ball skips down the fairway no further than 15 feet.

"You know, that was a lot better than I expected," the pro says. "Now, take the club out of your mouth and try with your hands."

What's the difference between a car tyre and 365 condoms?
One's a Goodyear, the other's a bloody great year.

Life sentence

A defence lawyer says to his client: "I've got good news and bad news. The bad news is your blood test came back and the DNA is an exact match with the sample found on the victim's shirt."

"Damn," says the client. "What's the good news?"

"Your cholesterol is down to 140."

Beastly business

A farmer wanted to have his hens 'serviced', and over a few ales in the local pub that night heard about a guy in the village who wanted to sell a rooster. The next day the farmer went to the man's house and bought the rooster. As he was leaving the guy shouted out, "Don't worry. That's the randiest bird you'll ever come across."

Sure enough, as soon as the farmer got the rooster into the yard it ran into the hen house and mounted each one in a flash. Then it ran into the barn and mounted all the horses. Then it went into the pig pen and did the same there.

The farmer tried to stop the rooster. "Stop!" he shouted. "You'll kill yourself!" But the rooster continued, seeking out each farm animal in turn.

The next morning the farmer looked out on the yard and saw the rooster, on his back with his legs in the air, and a buzzard hovering above. The farmer walked up to the rooster and said, "Look what you did. You killed yourself. Well, I did warn you."

Suddenly, the rooster opened an eye. "Shhhhh," it whispered. "That buzzard's getting closer."

How the other half lives

A priest and a nun are on their way back from the seminary when their car breaks down.

The garage doesn't open until morning, so they have to spend the night in a B&B. It only has one room available.

The priest says: "Sister, I don't think the Lord would object if we spend the night sharing this one room. I'll sleep on the sofa and you have the bed."

"I think that would be fine," agrees the nun. They prepare for bed, say some prayers and settle down to sleep.

Ten minutes pass and the nun says, "Father, I'm very cold."

"OK," says the priest, "I'll get a blanket from the cupboard."

Another ten minutes pass and the nun says again, "Father, I'm still terribly cold."

The priest says, "Don't worry; I'll get up and fetch you another blanket."

Another ten minutes pass, then the nun murmurs softly, "Father, I'm still very cold. I don't think the Lord would mind if we acted as husband and wife just for a night."

"You're right," says the priest. "Get your own blankets, woman."

Happiest days of your life

The children had all been photographed and the teacher was trying to persuade them each to buy a copy of the group picture.

"Just think how nice it will be to look at when you are all grown up and say, 'There's Jennifer; she's a lawyer,' or 'That's Michael; he's a doctor.'"

A small voice at the back of the room rang out, "And there's the teacher. She's dead."

Divine intervention

A Catholic priest and a nun are enjoying a rare round of golf on their day off. The priest steps up to the first tee and takes a mighty swing. He misses the ball entirely and says, "Sh*t, I missed."

The good Sister demands that he watches his language, but on his next swing, he does it again and shouts, "Sh*t, I missed."

"Father, I'm not going to play with you if you keep swearing," the nun complains.

The priest promises to hold his tongue, but on the fourth tee he misses again and can't stop cursing.

The Sister is really mad now and says, "Father John, God is going to strike you dead if you keep swearing like that."

On the next tee, Father John continues his bad form. Again he instinctively cries out, "Sh*t, I missed."

Suddenly a terrible rumble is heard and a gigantic bolt of lightning strikes Sister Marie dead in her tracks. Then, from the sky, a booming voice can be heard... "Sh*t, I missed!"

Only doing my job

The police chief was putting the new recruits through their paces and explaining to them how their new job might throw up some difficult issues. "For instance," he says, "what would you do if you had to arrest your wife's mother?"

One of the recruits raises his hand and says, "Call for back-up, sir."

Why do the French never play hide-and-seek?
Nobody wants to look for them.

Somebody up there likes me

The Chief Rabbi challenges the Pope to a game of golf.

The Pope then meets with the College of Cardinals to discuss the proposal. "Your Holiness," says one of the Cardinals, "I am afraid that this would tarnish our image in the world. You're terrible at golf."

"Don't we have a Cardinal to represent me?" says the Pope.

"There is a man named Jack Nicklaus, an American golfer, who is a devout Catholic. We can arrange to make him a Cardinal and then ask him to play as your personal representative," says the Cardinal.

Of course, Nicklaus is honoured and he agrees to play as a representative of the Pope.

The day after the match, Nicklaus reports to the Vatican to inform the Pope of the result. "I have some good news and some bad news, Your Holiness," says Nicklaus.

"Tell me the good news, Cardinal Nicklaus," says the Pope.

"Well, Your Holiness, I don't like to brag, but even though I have played some terrific rounds of golf in my life, this was the best I have ever played, by far. I must have been inspired from above."

"How can there be bad news, then?" the Pope asks.

"I lost by three strokes to Rabbi Woods," replies Nicklaus.

Clear my diary

When the new patient is settled comfortably on the couch, the psychiatrist begins his therapy session.

"I'm not aware of the nature of your problem," the doctor says, "so perhaps you should start at the very beginning."

"Of course," replies the patient. "In the beginning, I created the Heavens and the Earth."

Tonic for the troops

The soldiers are tired and lonely after spending weeks in enemy territory. To entertain them the Major calls for a dancer from the nearby town to entertain them. After the first dance, the soldiers go mad, clapping for five minutes.

For her second number she strips and dances in a sheer bra and G-string. This time the applause goes on for ten minutes. For her next number she dances topless and this time the applause goes on and on. The Major has to come on stage and ask them to quieten down for the grand finale.

For her last number, she strips completely and dances naked. The Major expects the soldiers to make enough noise to bring the roof down, but ten minutes later there is no clapping.

As the dancer comes offstage, the Major asks her, "What happened? How come there was no clapping this time?"

"How do you expect them to clap with one hand?" she says.

Now, you might feel a little prick

Two little boys, Sammy and Tom, are sharing a room in hospital.

As they're getting to know each other, Sammy asks, "What're you in for?"

"I'm getting my tonsils out. I'm a little worried," says Tom.

"Oh, don't worry about it," Sammy says. "I had my tonsils out and it was brilliant! I got to eat all the ice cream and jelly I wanted for two weeks!"

"Oh, yeah?" replies Tom. "That's not half bad. Hey, Sammy; how about you? What're you here for?"

"I'm getting a circumcision, whatever that is," Sammy answers.

"Oh, my God, circumcision? I had one of those when I was a baby and I couldn't walk for a year!" says Tom.

Better safe than sorry

Japan has banned all animal transport after discovering some nibbled beds in Tokyo.

They think it could be a case of Futon Mouse.

What do cookery books and science fiction have in common?

Men read them and think, "Well, that's not going to happen."

Employee relations manual

To cut costs, a managing director is forced to sack an employee. After much thought, he narrows the choice down to two young members off the office: Jack and Jill. As the pair have near-identical performance records, he cannot decide who should go, so, after hours of deliberation, he comes up with an idea; the first person to go for a fag break on Monday morning gets axed.

Monday arrives and Jill walks in with a monstrous hangover. After a few minutes, she heads outside for a cigarette. The director walks over. "Jill, I'm so sorry," he says, "but due to circumstances beyond my control, I've got to lay you or Jack off..."

"OK," replies Jill. "Would you just jack off, then? I've got a bloody awful headache this morning."

Bum steer

Three bulls, one large, one medium and one small, are standing in the pasture. They've just heard a rumour that the farmer is bringing in a new, larger bull.

The largest bull of the three says, "Well, he ain't getting none of my cows."

The medium bull says, "He ain't getting none of my cows."

So the little bull says, "Well, if he ain't getting any of yours, then he sure as hell ain't getting one of mine."

Two days later, a truck pulls into the yard and the farmer unloads the new bull. He's big and pissed off from having been cooped up for the long journey.

When the three bulls see him, the biggest bull says, "He can have my cows."

The medium bull says, "Yup, he can have mine, too."

The littlest bull, however, begins to paw the ground, snort and bellow.

"What the hell are you doing?" the other two ask.

"I'm just showing him I ain't a cow!"

Many a slip

A man enters hospital for a circumcision. The surgeons lie him down, put him to sleep and set to work on the job in hand. When the man comes to after the procedure, he's perturbed to see several doctors standing around his bed.

"Son, there's been a bit of a mix-up," admits the surgeon. "I'm afraid there was an accident and we were forced to perform a sex-change operation."

"What!" gasps the patient. "You mean I'll never experience another erection?"

"Oh, you might," the surgeon reassures him, "just not yours."

Looks like a vasectomy to me

After their 11th child a couple from Somerset decide that's enough. The husband goes to his doctor and tells him that he wants the snip.

"OK," says the doctor. "Go home, get a cherry bomb, light it, put it in a beer can, then hold the can up to your ear and count to ten."

The bumpkin replies, "I may not be the smartest man alive, but I don't see how putting a cherry bomb in a beer can next to my ear is going to help me."

So the man drives to London for a second opinion. The London physician is just about to explain the procedure for a vasectomy when he notices from the case file that the man is from Somerset. Instead the doc says, "Go home and get a cherry bomb, light it, place it in a beer can, hold it to your ear and count to ten."

The bumpkin figures that both doctors can't be wrong, so he goes home, lights a cherry bomb and puts it in a beer can. He holds the can up to his ear and begins the countdown.

"One, two, three, four, five...", at which point he pauses, places the beer can between his legs and resumes counting on his other hand.

What do you call ten lesbians in a closet?
A liquor cabinet.

Poultry and motion

Brian returns home from the pub late one night, stinking drunk. He gets into bed with his sleeping wife, gives her a kiss and nods off. When he awakes a strange man is standing at the end of his bed in a long flowing white robe.

"Who the hell are you?" demands Brian. "What are you doing in my bedroom?"

"This isn't your bedroom," the man answers, "and I'm St Peter".

Brian is stunned. "You mean I'm dead? That can't be; I have so much to live for! I haven't said goodbye to my family. You've got to send me back straight away!"

"Well you can be reincarnated," the holy man says, "but there's a catch. We can only send you back as a hen."

Brian's devastated, but knowing there's a farm near his house, he asks to be sent back right away. A flash of light later, he's covered in feathers and pecking the ground. Within minutes he feels a strange feeling welling up inside him.

The farmyard rooster strolls over and says: "I can see you're struggling, mate. Don't worry; you're ovulating. Just relax and let it happen. You'll feel much better." And so he does.

A few uncomfortable seconds later, an egg pops out from under his tail and an immense feeling of relief sweeps through him. When he lays his second egg, the feeling of happiness is overwhelming and he realises that being reincarnated as a hen is the best thing that has ever happened to him. The joy keeps coming but just as he's about to lay his third egg, he feels a massive smack on the back of his head and hears his wife shouting, "Brian, wake up you drunken b*stard! You're sh*tting the bed."

What do you call 300 white men chasing a black man?
The PGA tour.

Easy when you know

A woman arrives at the gates of Heaven. While she's waiting for St Peter to greet her, she peeks through the gates. She sees a beautiful banqueting table. Sitting all around are her parents and all the other people she has loved and who had died before her.

When St Peter comes by, the woman says to him, "This is such a wonderful place! How do I get in?"

"You have to spell a word," St Peter tells her.

"Which word?" the woman asks.

"Love."

The woman correctly spells 'Love' and St Peter welcomes her into Heaven.

About a year later, St Peter comes to the woman and asks her to watch the gates of Heaven for him that day. While the woman is guarding the gates, her husband arrives. "Darling, how have you been?" she asks.

"Oh, I've been doing pretty well since you died," her husband tells her. "I married the beautiful young nurse who took care of you while you were ill. We were on honeymoon and I went water-skiing. I fell and hit my head, and here I am. How do I get in?"

"You have to spell a word," the woman told him.

"Which word?" her husband asks.

"Antidisestablishmentarianism," she replies.

Double vision

A drunken old bloke stumbles into the front door of a pub, walks up to the barman and says, "Give me a damn shot of vodka."

The barman tells him that he's had enough, so the old guy swears and walks out of the front door.

A few minutes later, the same drunk comes in through the side door and stumbles up to the bar and demands a shot of vodka. The barman looks at him in disbelief and refuses to serve him again. The old man swears again and storms out.

Within minutes the same old bloke stumbles in through the back door and, before he can say a word, the barman says, "Listen, I told you twice already that I'm not going to serve you, so get out of my bar, you drunken bastard."

The old guy looks at the bartender and says, "Damn; how many bars do you work at?"

Smart thinking

An efficiency expert concludes his lecture with a note of caution.

"You need to be careful about trying these techniques at home," he says.

"Why?" asks a man in the audience.

"I watched my wife's routine at breakfast for years," the expert explains. "She made lots of trips between the fridge, cooker, table and cabinets, often carrying a single item at a time. One day I told her, 'Honey, why don't you try carrying several things at once?'"

"Did it save time?" the guy in the audience asked.

"Actually, yes," replies the expert. "It used to take her 30 minutes to make breakfast. Now I do it in ten."

Meeting his match

A scientist is sharing a train carriage from Norfolk to London with a farmer. To pass the time, he decides to play a game with the farmer.

"I'll ask you a question and if you get it wrong, you have to pay me a pound," says the scientist arrogantly. "Then you ask me a question and if I get it wrong, you get a tenner."

"You're on," says the farmer.

"OK; you go first," says the scientist.

The farmer thinks for a bit then says, "I know. What has three legs, takes ten hours to climb up a palm tree and ten seconds to get back down?"

The scientist is very confused and thinks long and hard about the question. Finally, the train is pulling into Waterloo. As it comes to a stop, the scientist takes out his tenner and gives it to the farmer.

"Well, you've got me stumped," says the scientist. "What does have three legs, takes ten hours to get up a palm tree and ten seconds to get back down?"

The farmer takes the tenner and puts it into his pocket. He then takes out a pound coin and hands it to the scientist.

"I don't know," he smiles.

Breathe deeply and relax

The phone at the local hospital rings and the duty medic picks it up to hear a man jabbering on the other end.

"My wife's contractions are only two minutes apart!" he says.

"Is this her first child?" the doctor asks.

"No, you idiot" the man shouts, "This is her husband!"

War is hell

At the start of WWI, a father tells his son he has to go and
fight for his country. Nodding, his son asks his father to bring
him back a German helmet from the battlefields. "You know,"
says the boy, "one with a spike on top."

And so, weeks later the man is out on the mud-soaked fields
of Flanders when he spies a German helmet lying in the mud.
Bending down to pick it up, he finds it stuck fast; as he grasps
the spike for a better grip, he realises there is a German soldier
still attached to it.

"If you pull me out of ze dirt, you can take me prisoner,"
says the soldier, through the mud.

"If I pull you out," says the Brit, "can I have your helmet for
my son?"

"Ja – be my guest!" the German replies.

But, after half an hour, he's still only managed to get the
Kraut out up to the waist. "I'm bloody knackered," he says,
catching his breath.

"Vud it help," replies the German soldier, "if I took my feet
out of ze stirrups?"

Better fold your tray table

A pompous priest is seated next to a redneck on a flight across
the US. After the plane is airborne, drink orders are taken.

"I'll have a Jack Daniels and Coke," says the redneck.

When it's the priest's turn to place his order he looks at the
redneck in disgust and says, "I'd rather be savagely raped by
brazen whores than let alcohol touch these lips."

The redneck hands his drink back to the flight attendant and
says, "Me, too. I didn't realise we had a choice!"

Speculate to accumulate

After his business goes bust, a redneck called Scooter finds himself in dire financial trouble and resorts to prayer. "God, please help me," he wails. "I've lost my business, and if I don't get some money, I'm going to lose my car as well. Please let me win the lottery."

Saturday night comes and Scooter watches aghast as someone else wins. Again, he begins to pray.

"God, please let me win the lottery! I've lost my business, my car and I'm going to lose my house."

Next Saturday night comes and Scooter still has no luck. Once again, he prays. "God, why haven't you helped me?" he cries. "I've lost my business, my house, my car and my children are starving! I've always been a good servant to you; please let me win the lottery just this once!"

Suddenly, there is a blinding flash of light as the heavens open and Scooter is confronted with the glowing, ethereal vision of God himself.

"Scooter," he booms. "Meet me half-way on this. Buy a ticket."

Thanks; I needed to hear that

Brazilian forward Ronaldo walks into a Burger King in Milan and asks for two Whoppers.

"OK," says the cashier. "You're not fat and you haven't lost it."

Heard about the new official Chelsea dartboard? It comes with no doubles or trebles.

Well, how about that?

An Aussie lass visiting Britain in February stops at a red light behind a trucker. She leaps out of her car, knocks on his window and says: "Hi, my name's Cheryl and you're losing your load."

The trucker shakes his head and drives on. At the next set of traffic lights, she stops behind him, gets out and taps on his window again saying, "Hi, I dunno if you heard me. My name's Cheryl and you're losing your load."

He drives on. At the third set of lights she's still tapping on his window, saying, "Hi, mate, my name's Cheryl and you're losing your load."

Once again he shakes his head and drives on.

At the fourth set of lights, the truck driver leaps out of his cab quickly, goes over to the blonde's car, taps on her window and says, "Hi, Cheryl. My name's Dave and I'm driving a gritter."

Accidents will happen

A redneck trucker is driving down the highway when he hears a loud thump under his rig. He stops to check the damage and then calls his boss.

"I hit a pig on the road and he's stuck under my truck," he explains. "What should I do?"

"Shoot him in the head," answers the boss. "Then pull him out and throw him in the truck."

The driver does it and then calls his boss back. "I did what you told me," he explains.

"So what's the problem?" snaps the boss.

The driver replies, "I don't know what to do with his motorcycle."

Members' enclosure

A group of second-, third- and fourth-year primary school kids are accompanied by two women teachers on a field trip to the local racetrack to learn about horses. Soon after arriving it's time to take the children to the toilet, so it's decided that the girls will go with one teacher and the boys with the other.

The teacher assigned to the boys is waiting outside the men's room, when one of the boys comes out and tells her that none of them can reach the urinal. Having no choice, she goes inside, helps the boys with their pants and begins hoisting the little boys up one by one to help them pee.

As she lifts one, she can't help but notice that he's unusually well endowed.

Trying not to show that she was staring, the teacher says, "You must be in the fourth."

"No, miss," he replies in a thick Irish brogue. "I'm in the seventh, riding Silver Arrow, but thanks for the fumble."

Scents and sensibility

Two Aussie girls walk up to the perfume counter in a superstore and pick up a sample bottle.

Shazza sprays it on her wrist and smells it: "That's quite nice, don't you think, Cheryl?"

"Yeah, what's it called?" says Cheryl to the assistant.

"Viens à moi," comes the reply.

"Viens à moi, what does that mean?" asks Shazza.

"Viens à moi, ladies, is French for 'come to me'," says the assistant haughtily.

Shazza takes another sniff and offers her arm to Cheryl saying, "That doesn't smell like come to me. Does that smell like come to you, Cheryl?"

172

Apart from that...

A man's eating lunch in a restaurant when he has cause to call the waiter over: "I've got some bad news and some worse news," he says. "Which do you want to hear first?"

The waiter opts to hear the bad news first.

"The bad news is there's a fly in my soup," says the diner.

"OK; what's the worse news?" enquires the waiter.

"It's the best part of the meal."

Man to man

A deaf mute strolls into a chemist's shop to buy a packet of condoms. Unfortunately the mute cannot see any of his required brands on the shelves and the chemist, unable to decipher sign language, fails to understand what the man wants. Frustrated, the deaf mute decides to take drastic action. He unzips his trousers and drops his penis on the counter, before placing a £5 note next to it. Nodding, the chemist unzips his own trousers, slaps his mammoth shlong down on the counter next to the mute's pecker, then picks up both notes and stuffs them in his pocket.

The now-furious deaf mute begins to grunt angrily at the chemist, waving his arms wildly.

"Sorry," says the chemist, shrugging his shoulders, "but if you can't afford to lose, you shouldn't gamble."

Way to go!

A man turns to his new girlfriend and says, "Since I first laid eyes upon your beautiful body, my darling, I've wanted to make love to you really, really badly."

The girlfriend responds, "Well, you succeeded."

Thanks for nothing!

Irish engineers Paddy and Shamus are standing at the base of a flagpole, looking up.

A blonde woman walks by and asks, "What are you doing?"

"We're supposed to find the height of the flagpole," says Shamus, "but we don't have a ladder."

The blonde takes a wrench from her purse, loosens a few bolts and lays the pole down. Next she pulls a tape measure from her pocket, takes a measurement and announces, "Five metres." She then walks away.

Paddy shakes his head and laughs. "Ain't that just like a blonde, Shamus? We ask for the height and she gives us the length!"

Gasoline Alley

A little girl asks her mother, "Mum, can I take the dog for a walk around the park?"

Mum replies, "No, because the dog's on heat."

"What does that mean?" asks the child.

"Go and ask your father. I think he's in the garage."

The little girl goes to the garage and asks, "Dad, may I take Susie for a walk around the block? I asked Mum, but she said that Susie was on heat, and to come and talk to you."

The dad thinks for a second. He then takes a rag, soaks it with petrol and scrubs the dog's rear end with it. "OK," he says, "you can go now, but keep Susie on the leash."

The little girl leaves. She returns a few minutes later with no dog on the leash.

"Hey, where's Susie?" the dad says.

"She'll be here in a minute," the little girl says. "She ran out of petrol and another dog's pushing her home."

Money well spent

One Saturday, an older man and a sexy brunette walk into an expensive fur store.

"Show the lady your finest mink coat!" the man tells the owner.

The owner retrieves the store's best mink. The young woman tries it on and loves it.

"Sir," the owner whispers to the man, "that fur costs £25,000."

"No problem," the man replies, "I'll write you a cheque."

"You can pick up the coat on Monday, after the cheque clears," the owner says.

On Monday, the man returns to the store on his own.

"How dare you show your face in here?" the owner screams. "There wasn't a penny in your account!"

"Yeah, sorry about that," the man says with a smile, "but I wanted to thank you for the best weekend of my life!"

Did you hear about the man who joined the nudist colony?
The first day was his hardest.

Mutually assured destruction

What's the difference between mechanical engineers and civil engineers?

Mechanical engineers build weapons; civil engineers build targets.

The finishing touch

A man's father dies, so he goes to the undertaker and tells him
he wants the best of everything for his dear old dad.

The man is so upset about his old man's death he can't bring
himself to go to the funeral. The next day, he gets a bill for
£8,000. He pays it. The next month, he gets another bill for £70.
He figures it's just a little supplementary bill, so he pays that, too.

Next month, another bill for £70 arrives, so he calls up
the undertaker and says, "I keep getting these bills for £70. I
thought I paid for the funeral already."

The undertaker says, "Well, you said you wanted the best for
your father, so I rented him a tux."

Cherchez la femme

Two men's shopping trolleys collide in a supermarket.

"Sorry," says the first man. "I was looking for my wife."

The second man replies, "Me, too. Let's work together. What
does yours look like?"

The first man describes his wife. "She's a tall brunette with a
great figure. What about yours?"

The second man thinks for a second, "She'll turn up. Let's
look for yours instead."

Textbook landing

Qantas Flight 101 is flying from Heathrow to Sydney, with
Shayne the pilot and Wayne the co-pilot. As they approach
Sydney airport, they look out of the front window.

"Christ," says Shayne. "Will you look how short that runway
is? This is going to be one of the trickiest landings you're ever
going to see!"

"You're not kidding, mate," replies Wayne.

"Right, Wayne, when I give the signal, you put the engines in full reverse," says Shayne.

So they approach the runway and as soon as the wheels hit the ground, Wayne slams the engines in reverse, puts the flaps down and stamps on the brakes. Amidst roaring engines, squealing tyres and lots of smoke, the plane screeches to a halt inches from the end of the runway, much to the relief of Shayne and Wayne and everyone on board.

As they sit in the cockpit regaining their composure, Shayne looks out of the front window and says to Wayne, "That has got to be the shortest runway I've ever seen in my whole life."

Wayne looks out the side window and replies, "Yeah, mate, but look how wide it is!"

Howdy, serif

Four fonts walk into a bar.

Barman says: "Oi! Get out! We don't want your type in here!"

Pin-sharp

An elderly gentleman had serious hearing problems for a number of years. He went to the doctor and was fitted with a set of hearing aids that allowed him to hear 100 per cent.

A month later, the gentleman went back for a check-up. The doctor said, "Your hearing's perfect. Your family must be really pleased for you."

The gentleman replied, "Oh, I haven't told my family yet. I just sit around and listen to the conversations. I've changed my will three times so far!"

Shaggy humps

Having just arrived at a Foreign Legion outpost, a raw recruit asks the corporal what the men do for recreation. The corporal smiles and says: "You'll see."

The young man is puzzled. "Well, you've got more than 100 men on this base and I don't see a single woman."

"You'll see," the corporal repeats.

That afternoon, 300 camels are herded into the corral. On a signal, the men go wild and sprint into the enclosure to grab a camel. The recruit sees the corporal hurrying past and grabs his arm.

"I don't understand," he says. "There must be over 300 camels and only 100 of us. Why is everybody rushing? Can't a man take his time?"

"What?" exclaims the corporal, wild-eyed. "And get stuck with an ugly one?"

I knew that!

President Bush is rehearsing his speech for the Beijing 2008 Olympic Games. He begins with "Ooo! Ooo! Ooo! Ooo! Ooo!"

Immediately, his speechwriter rushes over to the lectern and whispers in the president's ear: "Mr President, those are the Olympic rings. Your speech is underneath."

Old chap

An attractive woman from New York is driving through a remote part of Texas when her car breaks down. A few minutes later, a cowboy on horseback wearing leather chaps comes along.

"Howdy, ma'am. I'm Pete. Can I give you a ride into town?"

The woman accepts, climbs up behind him on the horse and they ride off.

Every few minutes, the cowboy lets out a whoop so loud that it echoes from the surrounding hills. When they arrive in town, he lets her off at a service station and yells one final "Yahoo!" before riding off.

"What did you do to get Pete so excited?" the service-station attendant asks.

"Nothing," she says, "I just sat behind him on the horse, put my arms around his waist and held on to his saddle horn so I wouldn't fall off."

"Lady," the attendant says, "apart from those chaps, Pete rides bareback."

Soft in the head

There are two old drunks in a bar. The first one says, "Ya know, when I was 30 and got a hard-on, I couldn't bend it with either of my hands. By the time I was 40, I could bend it about 10 degrees if I tried really hard. By the time I was 50, I could bend it about 20 degrees, no problem. I'm gonna be 60 next week and now I can almost bend it in half with just one hand"

"So," says the second drunk, "what's your point?"

"Well," says the first, "I'm just wondering how much stronger I'm gonna get!"

His hand in marriage

A man comes home from a poker game late one night and finds his wife waiting for him with a rolling pin.

"Where have you been?" she asks.

"Pack all your bags," he demands. "I lost you in a card game."

"How did you manage to do that?"

"It wasn't easy," he says. "I had to fold a royal flush."

Good enough for me

A local business is looking for office help. They put a sign in the window, stating: "HELP WANTED. Must be able to type, must be good with a computer and must be bilingual."

A short time afterwards, a dog trots up to the window and goes inside. He looks at the receptionist and wags his tail, then walks over to the sign, looks at it and whines. Getting the idea, the receptionist gets the office manager.

The manager says, "I can't hire you. The sign says you have to be able to type."

With that, the dog jumps down, goes to the typewriter and proceeds to type out a perfect letter.

The manager is stunned, but tells the dog, "The sign also says you have to be good with a computer."

The dog jumps down again and goes to the computer, where it enters and executes a spreadsheet perfectly.

By this time the manager is totally dumbfounded. He looks at the dog and says, "I realise that you are a very intelligent dog and have some interesting abilities. However, I still can't give you the job. You have to be bilingual."

The dog looks at the manager calmly and says, "Meow!"

Back in a mo

Cruising at 40,000 feet, an airplane suddenly shudders and a passenger looks out of the window. "Sh*t!" he screams, "one of the engines just blew up!"

Other passengers leave their seats and come running over. Suddenly the aircraft is rocked by a second blast as yet another engine explodes on the other side.

The passengers are in a panic now and even the stewardesses can't maintain order. Just then, standing tall and smiling confidently, the pilot strides from the cockpit and assures everyone that there is nothing to worry about. His words and his demeanour make most of the passengers feel better and they sit down as the pilot calmly walks to the door of the aircraft. There, he grabs several packages from under the seats and hands them to the flight attendants.

Each crew member attaches the package to their backs.

"Say," says an alert passenger, "aren't those parachutes?"

The pilot nods with a smile. The passenger goes on, "But I thought you said there was nothing to worry about?"

"There isn't," replies the pilot as a third engine explodes. "We're just going to get help."

What's black and white and tells the Pope to get lost?
A nun who's just won the lottery.

Love of his life

One day, a man came home early from work and was greeted by his wife dressed in very sexy lingerie and high heels. "Tie me up," she purred, "and you can do anything you want." So he tied her up and went golfing.

We can only do so much

Tony Blair is visiting an Edinburgh hospital. He enters a ward full of patients with no obvious sign of injury or illness and greets one.

The patient replies:

"Fair fa your honest sonsie face,
Great chieftain o' the puddin race,
Aboon them a' you take your place,
Painch, tripe or thairm,
As lang's my airm."

Blair is confused, so he just grins and moves on to the next patient and says hello.

The patient responds:

"Some hae meat and canna eat,
And some wad eat that want it,
But we hae meat and we can eat,
So let the Lord be thankit."

Even more confused, the PM moves on to the next patient, who immediately begins to chant:

"We sleekit, cowerin, timrous beasty,
Thou needna start awa sae hastie,
Wi' bickering brattle."

Now seriously troubled, Blair turns to the accompanying doctor and asks, "What kind of facility is this? A mental ward?"

"No," replies the doctor. "This is the serious Burns unit."

All heart

A big, burly man visited the local vicar's home and asked to see the vicar's wife, a woman well known for her charity work.

"Madam," he said in a broken voice, "I wish to draw your attention to the terrible plight of a poor family in this village. The father is dead, the mother is too ill to work and the nine children are starving. They are about to be turned on to the cold, empty streets unless someone pays their rent, which amounts to £400."

"How terrible!" exclaimed the vicar's wife. "May I ask who you are?"

"I'm their landlord," he sobbed.

Reality bites

The Three Bears returned one sunny Sunday morning from a stroll in the woods to find the door of their little house open. Cautiously, they went inside.

After a while, big Daddy Bear's deep voice boomed out, "Someone's been eating my porridge!"

Mummy Bear gave a yelp. "Someone's been eating MY porridge!" she said.

Little Baby Bear rushed in, "Forget the damn porridge, some b*stard's nicked the DVD player!"

That's telling him!

An Asian man walks into the currency exchange in New York City with 2000 yen and walks out with $72. The following week, he walks in with 2000 yen and is handed $66. He asks the teller why he got less money that week than the previous week.

The teller says, "Fluctuations, sir."

The Asian man storms out and, just before slamming the door, turns around and shouts, "Fluc you Americans, too!"

Virtue rewarded

A man is standing at the Pearly Gates before St Peter.

"All you need to have done is one good deed and we will allow you passage into heaven."

The man says, "No problem. I was stopped at a crossroads once and saw a gang of blokes harassing a young woman. I got out of my car, walked up to the leader, who was over seven feet tall and must have weighed nearly 15 stone, and I told him that abusing a woman is a cowardly act and that I would not tolerate it. I then reached up, yanked out his nose ring and kicked him in the balls to make a point."

St Peter is amazed and starts searching the man's life in his book in front of him and says, "I can't find that incident anywhere in your file. When did that happen?"

The man looks down at his watch and says, "Oh, about two minutes ago."

> What do you call an Amish guy with his hand up a horse's arse?
> A mechanic.

> Why should you never replace your sandwich toaster?
> Better the Breville you know.

Quick thinking

A university student delivers a pizza to an old man's house.

"I suppose you want a tip?" says the old man.

"That would be great," says the student, "but the other guy who does deliveries told me not to expect too much. He said if I got 50p, I'd be lucky."

The old man looks hurt. "Well, to prove him wrong, here's £5. What are you studying?"

"Applied psychology," replies the student.

Hot pursuit

Two Aussie girls, Sheila and Kylie, are out driving in a new sports car.

"Look out for cops," says Sheila. "I'm going to see how fast we can go."

After five miles of driving like Jenson Button Sheila looks across at Kylie and asks,

"Can you see any cops?"

"Yes," Kylie replies.

"Are their lights on?" says Sheila.

Kylie thinks for a moment, and then says, "Yes. No. Yes. No. Yes. No."

Drawing the line

An armless man walks into a bar, which is empty except for the bartender. He orders a pint of Guinness and, when he is served, asks the bartender if he would get the money from his wallet in his pocket, since he has no arms.

The bartender obliges him. He then asks if the bartender would tip the glass to his lips. The bartender does this until the man finishes his pint. He then asks if the bartender could get a hanky from his pocket and wipe the foam from his lips. The bartender does this, and comments that it must be very difficult not to have any arms and have to ask someone to do nearly everything for him.

The man says, "Yes, it is a bit embarrassing at times. By the way, where's your restroom?"

The bartender quickly replies, "The closest one is in the petrol station down the street."

Differential diagnosis

An attractive young girl, chaperoned by an ugly old lady, enters a doctor's office.

"We've come for an examination," says the young girl.

"All right," says the doctor. "Go behind that curtain and take your clothes off."

"No, not me," says the girl, "it's my old aunt here."

"Very well," says the doctor. "Madam, stick out your tongue."

No sprain, no gain

A man goes to his local gym to ask about yoga classes for beginners.

The instructor asks, "How flexible are you?"

"Well," replies the man, "I can't do Wednesdays."

Rabbiting in the headlights

An Essex girl was driving down the A13 when her car phone rang.

It was her boyfriend, urgently warning her, "Treacle, I just heard on the news that there's a car going the wrong way on the A13. Please be careful!"

"It's not just one car!" said the Essex girl. "There's hundreds of them!"

I asked you first

A copper pulls a guy over for speeding and notices his eyes are red.

He says, "Hello, sir. I see your eyes look red. Have you been drinking?"

The driver replies, "Hello, officer. I see your eyes look glazed. Have you been eating doughnuts?"

> **What did the fisherman say to the magician?**
> **"Pick a cod, any cod."**

Rash decision

Did you hear about the New Zealand farmer who thought he had an STD?

It turns out that he was just allergic to wool.

How many Frenchmen does it take to defend Paris?
It's never been tried.

Thanks anyway

A golfer is looking for a new caddy one day when his friend says, "I know a great caddy; he's 90 years old but he has eyes like a hawk."

"OK, then," says the man, "tell him I'm playing again in a week."

The week passes and they start to play. The golfer hits a perfect drive. He is so pleased with himself that he holds his follow-through position for several moments. Unwinding, he says to the caddy, "Did you see where it went?"

The caddy says, "I sure did."

"Great; where is it?"

The caddy replies, "I don't remember."

Double the fun

Why is the space between a woman's breasts and her hips called a waist?

Because you could easily fit another pair of breasts in there.

Quick learner

A customer at Morris' Gourmet Grocery marvelled at the proprietor's quick wit and intelligence.

"Tell me, Morris, what makes you so smart?"

"I wouldn't share my secret with just anyone," Morris replies, lowering his voice so the other shoppers won't hear, "but, since you're a good and faithful customer, I'll let you in on it. Fish heads: you eat enough of them, you'll be positively brilliant."

"You sell them here?" the customer asks.

"Only £4 apiece," says Morris.

The customer buys three. A week later, he's back in the store complaining that the fish heads were disgusting and he isn't any smarter.

"You didn't eat enough," says Morris.

The customer goes home with 20 more fish heads. Two weeks later, he's back and this time he's really angry.

"Hey, Morris," he says, "you're selling me fish heads for £4 apiece when I just found out I can buy the whole fish for £2. You're ripping me off!"

"You see?" says Morris. "You're smarter already."

Fanny peculiar

A coachload of OAPs is out on a day trip travelling around the country. Suddenly, without warning, one of the old ladies leaps into the air."I've just been molested!" she screams.

The coach driver stops the coach, "But we're down a country lane in the middle of nowhere!" he says. "Did any one else see anything?"

All the other old folk on the coach shake their heads and, as things settle down, the driver heads off again.

A couple of miles along the road, the same old lady leaps into the air, "I've been molested again! Stop the coach!"

This time, the driver, wondering if she might be a little bit senile, walks back to her seat and has a look underneath.

To his amazement, there's an old, bald chap curled up in the footwell, squinting up at him.

"What the hell are you doing?" asks the driver.

"I haven't got my glasses and I'm looking for my toupée," the old geezer replies. "I almost had it twice, but it got away both times!"